b

Libra
nam

RIVER, RAILWAY AND RAVINE

FOOT SUSPENSION BRIDGES FOR EMPIRE

RIVER, RAILWAY AND RAVINE

FOOT SUSPENSION BRIDGES FOR EMPIRE

DOUGLAS HARPER

First published 2015

The History Press
The Mill, Brimscombe Port
Stroud, Gloucestershire, GL5 2QG
www.thehistorypress.co.uk

British Library Cataloguing in Publication Data.
A catalogue record for this book is available from the British Library.

ISBN 978 0 7509 6213 1
Typesetting and origination by The History Press
Printed in China

For Tom Day (1936–2014)
Friend and Mentor

Cover illustrations: *Front*: Bridge erected near Bombay (Mumbai).
(Aberdeen Art Gallery & Museums Collections); *rear*: Bridge over the
River Ericht. (Aberdeen Art Gallery & Museums Collections)

CONTENTS

FOREWORD

The design, development and construction of lightweight suspension footbridges may seem an unlikely topic to stir the imagination but, when considering the progress made on such bridges by John Harper and his son Louis, it was significant.

By 1860 the Aberdeen firm of Harper & Co. – iron gate maker and wire manufacturers – had been established, and John Harper had registered a patent for a mechanism to tension the wire fences that can still be seen adjacent to our modern railways. The system, with its hand-cranked mechanism, was then adapted to tension the catenary wire cables of the lightweight suspension bridges that the Harpers built throughout north-east Scotland, the United Kingdom and the British Empire.

A number of these bridges still exist and remain in use. However, many have suffered the ravages of time, and have decayed, especially those where timber pillars were used as the main part of the bridge structure.

One factor that is particularly refreshing about this account of the Harpers' bridge-building activities is the author's enthusiasm and dedication, particularly when describing his, and sometimes his family's, search of overgrown river banks and more distant places that once were the site of a Harpers' bridge.

Tom Day
Engineer & Historian

ACKNOWLEDGEMENTS

Much of the content of this book revolves around the Harper archive at the Aberdeen Museum, and I am indebted to Mike Dey and Jenny Brown of that museum for their encouragement and assistance. I am also indebted to the staff of the Kemnay branch of the Aberdeenshire Libraries, Aberdeenshire Heritage, Aberdeenshire Council, Aberdeen Central Library, the Aberdeen Archivist, the Library of the University of Aberdeen, the Dundee Archivist, Hertfordshire County Council, the Moray Archive, the National Library of Scotland, particularly its Map Room, the National Archives of Scotland, the Record Offices at Chester, Matlock, Derbyshire, Yorkshire and Carlisle, Manfred Keenleyside of the Falklands Island Museum, Carol Morgan of the Institution of Civil Engineers, George Dixon of Grantown Museum, and Eddie Groggan of Bandon.

Landowners have always been most approachable and I thank the Factor, Balmoral Estate, Viscount and Viscountess Long of Newquay, Lord Crathorne of Yarm, North Yorkshire, Sir Archibald Grant of Monymusk, Marcus Humphries of Aboyne, Mr & Mrs Rattray of Craighall and Mr & Mrs Taylor of Banchory. Many individuals have given generously of their time to search and provide information, including Eric Baird and Mike Martin of the Glentanar Ranger Service, Duncan Downie, Kemnay, Jeff Taylor of Keswick, Rob Hale, Helen and Linda Arthan of Shocklach Green; John Ross, Charles Nichol, Kareen Edwards, Pat Knox and Dr Pierre Fouin, Aberdeen, Professor Douglas Maxwell, London, Makila Brown, K. Dixit, Professor Manohar Shrestha, and Santan Arjyal, Kathmandu, Julija Maltseva, Narva, Estonia, Professor Colin O'Connor, Brisbane, Tim Devine, Doveridge and Alan Johnston, North Berwick. Photographs are individually attributed, otherwise they are the author's.

At an early stage in my quest I was fortunate to meet the late Dr Tom Day, recently retired from Robert Gordon University. It was he that suggested that this record be made and he has been a constant source of encouragement and information throughout. The preparation of various drafts has been enhanced by advice from Laughton Johnston and my children Caroline, Lorraine, Ross and Helen, for which I am most grateful. Wendy Simpson undertook the task of editing the manuscript and it is much the better for her efforts. However, as a non-engineer there will be many errors of fact and interpretation for which I take full responsibility. My wife Janette has been my constant companion throughout the entire gestation – in the field at home and abroad, in museums and libraries and at home. I cannot thank her enough. I also wish to thank Amy Rigg, Lauren Newby and their colleagues at The History Press for their enthusiasm, patience and professionalism.

Finally, I am grateful for the financial support towards the publication of this book provided by Elspeth Barrack (formerly Harper) of Knight Property Group, Aberdeen.

Douglas Harper

INTRODUCTION

In all man's attempts to control his environment, it is the bridge which brings most excitement and acclaim. Some will only see their utility, others their beauty but to all, the completion of a bridge heralds a new chapter in the history of the area. From a felled tree across a stream, the aqueducts of Rome and the chain suspension bridges of the early nineteenth century, to the giant long spans of the twentieth century, there has been a constant competitive evolution. They are the highest form of the civil engineers' art. They change the world – whatever its size.

Of all bridges, it is the suspension bridge that appeals most to the imagination. What is their magic? Is it because the supporting structure is highly visible and the tower height, the sweep of the deck and the curve of the cable never fails to draw the eye? Light, airy, elegant and graceful are all epithets you will come across in this account. Their elegance is matched by their economy and the speed of their construction and, for this reason, they often found a role in developing countries. Suspension bridges saved lives, facilitated trade and allowed neighbouring communities to mix and merge.

The earliest suspension bridges on record were found in the eastern Himalayas where they were seen by Chinese travellers. They in turn took the idea to South America. Sporadic constructions in Europe followed similar travellers' tales, between 1660 and 1800. After a very productive period of foot suspension bridge building in the UK in the early nineteenth century, there was something of a hiatus until the later years of that century. It was during that period, around 1870, that John Harper emerged as a bridge builder, embracing a simple technology that deserves to be better known. The Harpers were pioneers in the use of steel wire rope in their bridges which they exported in kit form to all corners of the globe.

In my childhood I remember a large box in the garage from which was occasionally withdrawn, with much care, a beautiful model of a foot suspension bridge. At some stage it went off to a museum, as did some photographs of the bridges of my grandfather and great grandfather. In recent years I became curious about the whereabouts of the model bridge and, as I thought that it had gone to the museum of the Robert Gordon University, Aberdeen, I made contact with the people there. They knew nothing about it, but they did know something of Harpers' bridges, a topic used for student projects. They had a list of bridges; so had I but the two lists didn't match, so our joint list doubled to about a dozen. Just how many had there been, and did any of them still exist?

My first port of call was the Aberdeen Maritime Museum. There I studied the photographs and other archival material. In all there were about fifty photographs of bridges, usually annotated on the reverse by my great-grandfather or his son. Many of them were attached to press cuttings that related to the openings of the bridges illustrated.

However, challenges remained – for example, there were, and still are, several rivers Dee and place names were often spelled differently than in today's maps. National borders had changed and a feature crossed by a bridge may have moved or no longer exist. The local press, wherever a bridge had been built, were invariably helpful either from their own archive or correspondence columns. The establishment of a website (www.harperbridges.com) continues to turn up new contacts with information. Examples of business stationery, testimonials from clients and family correspondence also helped to fill out some detail. The study of contemporary maps was always rewarding, giving clues not only to location, but also to an idea of the wider scene, the size and importance of settlements and modes of communication. Comparison with an up-to-date map revealed either that the footbridge had been replaced by a road bridge, or had been removed, or was still the site of a footbridge. If the latter, was it an original Harper bridge or a replacement?

Field work followed when there was nothing for it but to go and see for ourselves. Accompanied by my wife and occasionally grandchildren, we scoured railway embankments, scrambled along gorges and trudged along miles of river bank throughout the UK, in Africa and the Indian subcontinent – a great way to see our country and the wider world. We spent hours in libraries and archives from Australia to Aberdeenshire searching for clues. Often we were too late; other times there were some remains such as an anchorage, footings, ironwork or abutment, and occasionally the reward of a Harper suspension bridge still in use. On the way we learned about the development of the design of the bridges over the years and more about the men who made them. In all, we now have knowledge of at least sixty bridges worldwide and there were almost certainly several more. What was the effect of the Harpers' endeavours?

This account is a record of the bridges built by a medium-sized family foundry in nineteenth century Aberdeen, in north-east Scotland. The story of this family's industry is a reflection of the times. The company grew from a maker of wrought iron gates and fences to a manufactory of machinery and motor cars, as well as suspension bridges. I have confined myself largely to their innovative bridge building derived from their fencing and have tried to address the historical, political, social or economic contexts surrounding each bridge. This book may appeal to local historians in north-east Scotland and wherever a bridge was built. It aims to fill a gap in the nineteenth century record of the development of these bridges and so might be of interest to industrial archaeologists. Finally, it is written without any knowledge or background in engineering and so is non-technical and aimed mainly at the general reader.

Now let us meet the 'makers' John Harper and his son Louis.

1

FROM DEVERON TO DEE

Fan I was only ten year old I left the parish schweel,
My Faither he fee'd me tae the Mains to chaw his milk and meal
(G.S. Morris)

Rural north-east Scotland in the early nineteenth century was a hard place in which to grow up. Large families were an economic necessity in times when infant mortality was so high. Rural communities were on the move to the towns and cities, following cottage industries to the new factories. Poverty and fresh air were exchanged for poverty and stench, a poor diet of what could be grown for a poor diet of what could be bought and the security of extended families for the solitariness of the crowd. For those who remained it was a life of unremitting toil. Until the early nineteenth century, the mobility of the population had been minimal. Roads were poor and transport was most probably by cart. People stayed put, perhaps straying across a parish boundary to seek work or a wife or husband, but little further.

To our knowledge there have been Harpers in north-east Scotland since the early fourteenth century. They first appear with lands on the 'sunny side of Methlick' at the time of the Wars of Independence and they married into the Gordons of Haddo, whose coat of arms of the time included a clàrsach or harp to remind us of the union.[1]

In the fourteenth century the trail goes cold, but in the mid-eighteenth century the Harpers re-emerge as a notable family in the parish of Marnoch, some 35 miles (56km) west-north-west of Aberdeen on the left bank of the River Deveron. According to local author and historian Fenton Wyness, given the small size of communities and lack of mobility

of the times, the family's connection with the Methlick heartland, only 15 miles (24km) away, is 'almost certain'. This relationship with Marnoch is reinforced by the name given to a local hill within the parish and the farm on it: Harperhill. The names of physical features often date back centuries; so who was the Harper after whom the hill was named and when did this appellation stick? Harperhill is in sight of the Inverkeithny graveyard where so many Harpers now lie. Although today the road journey from Harperhill to Inverkeithny is 6 miles (9.6km), in the eighteenth century a ferry across the Deveron provided a direct link. The ferryman's cottage and the road that passes it down to the riverbank can still be seen.

John Harper's father, Hugh, farmed at Mill of Laithers, a few miles downstream towards Turriff on the right bank of the Deveron. Hugh was born in 1805 in the parish of Marnoch. In 1831, described as a farmer/gardener, he married Margaret Hall, from King Edward just north of Turriff, who was two years his senior. Later that year, their eldest son, also named Hugh, was born, followed two years later, in 1833, by John, the central character in this story.

John Harper's paternal grandfather was another John (born 1770) and was also a farmer, possibly from Banff, who married Elspet Pirie (born 1766) from Marnoch. John and Elspet married in 1787 and went on to have a family of nine. We do not know exactly where the Harper family lived and worked, but they are likely to have made their home in

1. The Harper family tree, with the Mill of Laithers nestling in the Deveron Valley, Aberdeenshire.

a heather-thatched 'but an' ben' somewhere in the parish of Marnoch. We know that when they were in their 70s John and Elspet resided at Millbrex, Fyvie and that John died in 1842. In the 1851 census[2] Elspet, on her own, is described as a 'domestic servant, pauper'. She died in 1860 at Aberchirder, Marnoch's main village, aged 94 years.

Elspet and John's son, Hugh, had made his mark to the extent that he had become an overseer with the Ardmiddle Estate (nowadays he would be employed as a farm manager). His own family consisted of Hugh, John, Peter and Charles. Today, the view over the Deveron valley near Mill of Laithers shows acres of barley rippling in the breeze, well-kept farmhouses and older farm buildings that have been converted to modern homes. The area is well tended, fertile and relatively prosperous. This prosperity has been built upon the backbreaking efforts put into draining, boulder clearing, ploughing and sowing by men and horses of previous generations. The name 'Laithers' appears in many local farms and also applies to a castle on which the old land of Laithers was presumably centred. Much of the farm, as it was built in the early nineteenth century, remains unchanged today. Past the house flows the Muiresk Burn along which, in earlier times, were a series of mills,

including flour and sawmills. The young Harpers most likely went to school in Turriff, 2 miles (3.2km) away.

The four Harper boys would have had a great time growing up at Mill of Laithers. The Muiresk Burn that flowed through the farm and the several mills that lay on its course, must have provided plenty of scope for mischief and there would have been trout and salmon to be caught in the Deveron nearby. The boys would have had friends aplenty among the families of the cottar houses and in the family that lived at Mill of Muiresk at the top of the road.

Each morning and afternoon would take them past the Mill of Muiresk on their way to Turriff and to school. Once home, the boys would have had duties around the farm; they would have helped with milking, with feeding the animals and mucking out the byre. In season, there would be a harvest to bring in or tatties (potatoes) to pick. Children brought up on Aberdeenshire farms in the early part of the nineteenth century would have worked hard and played hard until, all too soon, at the grand age of 9, their schooldays were over; it was time to be 'fee'd' (or hired). In the 1841 census[3] when he would have been all of 10 years old, Hugh is not listed as a resident at Mill of Laithers, but in the household of the minister at Forglen, 5 miles (8km) to the north-east, as a servant. In 1851, he is recorded as an apprentice in the barley trade at Mill of Towie, Auchterless, 6 miles (9.6km) south of Mill of Laithers.[2] Ten was a not uncommon age for a boy to leave home to be apprenticed. Local author Hunter Diack, writing of the same time, tells us of his father being apprenticed to a Kemnay tailor at that age, and we are also reminded by the quoatation at the beginning of this chapter of G.S. Morris's bothy ballad of about 1880, 'A Pair o' Nicky Tams', describing the hiring of its 10-year-old narrator.

John, Hugh's younger brother, left home at the age of 9.[4] In his youth he trained in market and landscape gardening, moving around the area, perhaps including the parish of Culsalmond. Also in that parish was an Eliza Wilson, who had a daughter, Eliza (Lizzie) in 1852, when she was 16 years of age. About this time John, presumably the father of her child, headed south with his brother Hugh to Edinburgh. Had John been under pressure to marry Eliza and hence made himself scarce? Or did he wish to improve his position before returning to marry her? Either way the brothers left the north-east around late 1851 and returned in 1856. In the intervening five years they were in Edinburgh and then Glasgow. It was in Edinburgh that they became fencers and, at some time during the period 1852–54, John found himself to have the confidence required to

2. Mill of Laithers today.

lead industrial action, according to an interview he gave to the *Northern Figaro* in 1886.[4] John returned to marry Eliza in 1854 and, at about this time, he moved to Glasgow, where the couple established a home at 17 Eglington Place, Laurieston, on the south side. Their son John was born the following year. It is interesting to note that, on the birth certificate, John contrived to have the date of their marriage advanced by two years, to just before the arrival of their daughter Eliza! By this time, John senior was manager of a large fencing works, possibly those of nearby P. & R. Fleming.

In the middle of the nineteenth century Glasgow was booming as the second city of the Empire. Railways were extending in all directions and the Clyde shipyards were embracing the iron technology that was fast replacing timber. The iron furnaces of Lanarkshire and Carron were fed by the coalfields of the midland valley of Scotland. Tobacco, sugar and cotton from the Empire landed at the city's quays. However, as exciting as Glasgow no doubt was in the 1850s, city life had a downside. Within a year or two, cholera had claimed the lives of 4,000 citizens, mainly children and the elderly, while tuberculosis was rife. Eliza contracted tuberculosis and it may be that her illness played a part in John and Hugh's decision to return to Aberdeen, to a more amenable environment and their 'ain folk'. Sadly she died in Aberdeen the following year, at the age of 21, leaving two young children.

In 1850 the railway arrived in Aberdeen from the south and this brought markets nearer, particularly for meat and fish, but also for paper. These were major industries which were hampered by the distance from major markets. Previously, cattle had been moved south by drovers or by sea but now both live and dead meat could be rapidly transported to the south. Fish, stored in ice, could be similarly transported to central Scotland and to London.

John arrived back to a thriving Aberdeen in 1856, in the middle of a century of change.[5] At the opening of the century, the city had developed two huge thoroughfares which overlay the medieval town and allowed it to develop far beyond its boundaries. These were Union Street and King Street. Union Street was named after the Union of Great Britain and Ireland. It was laid out to the west of the Castlegate, cutting through the northern half of St Katherine's Hill and then rising on arches over the slope to the north of the Green, bridging the routes passing north from

the Green. It then crossed the great dip of the Denburn valley by way of the Union Bridge, the greatest granite single-span bridge of the time. Beyond the bridge, the thoroughfare gained the open ground where the Music Hall now stands and allowed the development of today's West End. King Street headed north towards the separate town of Old Aberdeen and a new Don crossing.

Growth round these great streets was slow, however, due to economic circumstances. In the 1840s, Aberdeen's large textile industry, which had employed half the city's workforce, fell on hard times as a result of owners speculating on the railways and other factors. All but four of the great mills closed. However, as the textile mills failed, so the paper mills grew, often using the same power sources and even buildings. These were mainly found on the banks of the River Don or on minor streams and lades within the town, particularly along the Den Burn and in Gilcomston to the north-west of the city centre. Indeed, the Broadford Mill closed only a few years ago and papermaking continues at Stoneywood to this day.

London was also the target of the granite industry – for decades the streets of the capital had been surfaced with granite setts from Aberdeenshire quarries. Around 1830, granite polishing had come in, giving rise to a secondary memorial stone industry. As Aberdeen developers emulated Edinburgh's New Town this beautiful stone was used in both the public and private buildings designed by architects such as Archibald Simpson (1790–1847), John Smith (1781–1852) and Alexander Marshall Mackenzie (1848–1933). To the west, beyond the Den Burn lay the residential area with villas for the professionals and well off in Union Street, Golden and Bon Accord Squares and Albyn Place. However, grand though many of these buildings were, the vast majority of the 75,000 population were still living crammed into the confines of the medieval city, with the harbour and estuary of the Dee at its commercial heart.

By 1860, the shipyards were flourishing and while Glasgow was developing its iron and steel ships, close as it was to these raw materials, Aberdeen stayed longer with wooden construction and perfected the sailing clipper for long haul of grain, tea, wool and opium. Walter Hood & Co. launched the *Thermopylae* in 1868, a vessel that was to become the fastest sailing ship afloat, taking sixty-three days on her maiden voyage to Melbourne, a record never beaten (covering a record 380 miles (608km) in a day's sail).[6] The age of the clipper started at around 1839 and lasted until the opening of the Suez Canal in 1869. During this period Alexander Hall & Co. built 290 and Walter Hood 40 of these great sailing ships. So by the 1860s Aberdeen was growing and thriving again after the lean 1840s.

To the south, the River Dee had been directed to its intermediate course through the inches (following the line of today's Albert Basin) to allow for the laying out of Market Street and the railhead. Still quite separate were the districts we know today as Rosemount, Kittybrewster, Woodside, Old Aberdeen, Ferryhill, Torry and Mannofield.

In 1856, John went into partnership with Frier as Harper, Frier & Co., at 82 King Street, with works at 187 King Street and, later, close by in Farrier Lane. By the next year the company was simply Harper & Co., Iron Gate and Wire Manufacturers. By this time John had been joined by his brothers Hugh and Peter. As Harper & Co., in 1861 the brothers moved around the corner to 8–14 Mealmarket Street, maintaining a shop at 82 Union Street. Usually the business had two addresses, one of them being the shop through which contracts were made and goods displayed. The public did not normally access the second address, the works or 'manufactory'. All these addresses were well within the boundaries of the old town and commercial centre, all within a half-mile radius of one another. The Mealmarket Street works were probably quite limited, but nevertheless it was here that the fortunes of the firm grew. Harper & Co.'s main fencing contracts for the Great Indian Peninsula Railway (GIPR), the Great North of Scotland Railway (GNSR) and several highland estates were completed and exported from the Mealmarket Street foundry. Great opportunities for fencing lay in the agricultural hinterland – particularly in the Moray and Kincardineshire areas where there was a great expansion of wire fencing in the 1860s and 1870s.[7] Initially, John Harper maintained a residence at or adjacent to the works on Mealmarket Street, but by 1868 the family had moved to a top floor flat at 115 Union Street. John, a widower for five years with two young children, found himself his second wife, Margaret Ross, in 1862. A third child, Louis, was born to them in 1868. This address was to remain in the family until the 1920s as the office initially for the Harper Bridge Co., later merely Louis Harper, AMICE, Architect and Civil Engineer, and then for Harper & Sutherland, Architects and Civil Engineers. However, increasing business success and prosperity allowed John and Hugh to relocate in the country west of Aberdeen, where John was to purchase the lands of Seafield in 1872.

What exactly underpinned the success of this developing business? The answer, we will find, lay in a small and disarmingly simple invention.

2

POST AND WIRE

The pillar in each case is cast or formed hollow, and contains the
whole of the gearing or straining apparatus.
(From John Harper's Patent Specification, 1863)

To understand the genesis of Harpers' bridge-building enterprise, we must first understand their fencing business.

The middle decades of the nineteenth century were prosperous for farmers in most places, and the north-east of Scotland was no exception.[7] This allowed them to improve the farm infrastructure such as buildings and fencing. While certain areas had a sufficiency of field boulders to allow enclosure by dry stone dykes, much of Buchan had to await the introduction of wire fencing in mid-century. The country areas underlain by granite or glacial boulder clay produced enough boulders to ensure dry stone dyking, but wide areas of the Buchan plateau were inadequately fenced. Similarly, the sandstone areas of the Moray lowlands and southern Kincardineshire had rich soils derived from the softer old red sandstone, with fewer boulders as a result. By 1880 the Laigh of Moray was fully enclosed, almost wholly by wire fences, and the same was true of Kincardineshire, wire fencing being half the price of paling fencing, the only alternative. In the 1880s, Harpers were the largest fencers in the area.

As well as solving an agricultural problem, this innovation had another important social consequence. Until enclosure, livestock had to be herded by children for much of the year. Following enclosure, children were freed to attend school, particularly after it was made compulsory in 1872. An insight into the life of one herd boy is found in Charles Murray's poem *The Whistle*.[8] Having crafted the whistle, the boy could be heard all day as he looked after the livestock:

He wheepled on't at mornin'and he tweedled on't at nicht,
He puffed his frecked cheeks until his nose sank oot o'sicht.

However, as a result of either the turn of the seasons or the march of progress, including perhaps a Harpers' fence, he had to exchange the freedom of the fields for the confinement of the schoolroom. What was far worse, however, was the loss of his whistle to the schoolmaster's fire!

In addition, the railway had reached Aberdeen from the south in 1850 and, over the next two decades, the GNSR spread its tentacles over the north-east. All of these track beds had to be fenced, usually by Harpers.

John and Hugh Harper had acquired the necessary skills in their years in Central Scotland. 'They didna learn their fencing here,' says Duncan Mitchell, the family's current successor at Mill of Laithers, 'for there's naethin' here but dry stane dykes.' Dry stane dyke building in north-east Scotland represented an act of making a virtue out of necessity for the fields were constantly being cleared of boulders by generations of farm workers. The Harper brothers would have learned their fencing while working in Central Scotland. Had John Harper perhaps visited the north-east as an employee of his Glasgow 'large fencing works'[9] and then decided to return and set up his own business in Aberdeen?

In Glen Tanar there is iron gatework, which is probably of an earlier date than the Harper fencing, that bears the name P. & R. Fleming, Glasgow. In its day this was a prominent fencing firm based at the east end of Argyll Street with works in Stockton Street. John and Eliza lived a stone's throw away in Eglington Place. It is tempting to suggest that John was in Fleming's team up on the hills above Glen Tanar and saw an opportunity to return to Aberdeen and start his own business.

John and Hugh established the company's new works in Mealmarket Street in 1861 and stayed until 1879, during which time they were joined by their brother Peter as blacksmith. Previously they had been fencers, iron gate and wire manufacturers, so that working wrought iron, welding and drawing wire may have been the main activities in the earlier works in King Street and Farrier Lane, dating back to 1857. It is possible that they began to cast their own components from iron pigs (the product of the blast furnace) only on their move to Mealmarket Street. Here they developed their hollow cast iron fence posts and later the capability to cast larger bridge components, including the pillars for bridges such as that at Ravenscraig, Dundee (10ft 6in; 3.20m) in 1872. From this foundry came most of the fences supplied by the company for railways both at home and abroad, as well as level-crossing gates, and gates and fences for local estates, all of which combined to serve as the basis of a successful enterprise.

Harper & Co. was the most prominent of companies operating in the fencing trade in north-east Scotland by 1886.[4] During the 1860s to 1880s, the company fenced much of the local GNSR system and many of its cast iron fence posts survive to this day. They can still be seen along the Deeside line, the Speyside Way, near the Cullen Viaduct and elsewhere in the system.

3. Harper strainer post. Note the wires are closer together lower down the post.

4. Detail of the Harper straining device within the fence post.

Much of the success of the Mealmarket Street Foundry can be attributed to the invention of the Harper fence strainer, patented in 1863.[10] The strainer post illustrated is seen to include six wire-tensioning devices, each able to rotate on an axis at right angles to the wire, which passed through the outer casing and was then wound onto the rotating spindle. The wire was wound within the post using a crank handle rather like an Allen key. Once the operator had achieved the tension he desired, the spindle could be locked by inserting a peg or key into each of a pair of notches, one on the spindle and the other on the casing. This method resembled the process of fixing a wheel to its axle by inserting a key into slots prepared in both components and represented a technique frequently used in general foundry work of the time. John Harper filed the patent for his 'device for straining wire' in December 1863. It is interesting that the notches on the spindle were at 60-degree intervals, whereas those on the casing were at 90-degree intervals. This means that if the operator rotated the spindle only 30 degrees, he would be able to insert the locking key into a new pair of notches. This was an elegant solution to the challenge posed by the need to reduce as much as possible the increments by which tension could be increased, while avoiding making so many notches in each component that the strength of the cast

would be compromised. No specific mention was made of this intriguing technique in the patent specification and it is possible that the method was then in general use. Harper & Co. was certainly not the only fencer in Aberdeen at the time.

Joseph Rowell, a blacksmith based in the Rosemount area of Aberdeen, had successfully applied for a patent for a similar device the previous year.[11] He made a further application for a modified apparatus the following year, September 1863.[12] However, although there were similarities between the Harper and Rowell models, John Harper's apparatus was designed to enclose the winding mechanism and thus to protect it from the elements. A detailed comparison of the Rowell and Harper posts of the time is reported elsewhere.[13] Moreover, when John Harper submitted his application for the patent of his 'device for straining wire' in 1863, he mentioned not only fencing, but also the tensioning of telegraph lines, thereby aligning his device with some of the newest technology of the time.

In the 1860s, an important market for fences was the railways. As the railway network extended its web across the country, in many cases it crossed the roads that had previously represented the only routes in and out of most towns. Because of this there was a demand for rather splendid level-crossing

5. An example of a level crossing gate, this one at Peterhead. (*Aberdeen Art Gallery & Museums Collections*)

6. Harper strainer post showing the base plate and fins.

gates to be mounted on large, hollow, cast iron posts. Illustrated is the former level-crossing gate at Peterhead. A splendid example can still be seen at the entrance to Broomhill Station on the Strathspey Railway (transferred from the former Nethybridge Station across the valley). Memorabilia, such as maker's plates, command high prices at auction today. I have been asked to comment on the provenance of one such plate which was sold at auction in the south of England for £120.

Estates in north-east Scotland fenced by Harper & Co. include the Glenfiddich and Glenlivet Estatse in Speyside and the Glentanar Estate in Deeside. In the latter, Harpers' gates and fences were still very much in evidence in the 1870s and took the form of wire fences stapled to timber posts, with periodic cast iron runner or intermediate posts (a slimmer, simpler version of the strainer posts but without the winding apparatus), the whole being tensioned by the strainer posts at corners or boundaries. Elsewhere, nearer the big house, iron bars replaced the wire horizontals. The fence posts usually measured 7ft 3in (2.21m) in total height, about 4ft (1.22m) of which remained above ground. However, much of Glen Tanar was enclosed by a deer fence variant, about a foot higher.

7. Post in a deer fence in Glen Tanar.

Harper & Co., in common with all of Aberdeen's foundries, developed a thriving export business – in the case of Harpers, this was with India. Contracts let by the India Office in London were won and the goods dispatched by sea from Aberdeen. The British, in the latter part of the nineteenth century, were also heavily involved in the building of the Argentinean railways and it wouldn't be surprising if fencing contracts followed. However, there is as yet no evidence of Harpers exporting to South America.

Harper & Co.'s most notable fencing contract in India was for the Nagpur Extension of the GIPR. The Public Works Department in India was founded in 1850 by Lord Dalhousie, Viceroy of India from 1848 to 1856, to advance the development of roads, railways and canals in British India.[14] Amongst its projects were the Ganges Canal and the GIPR. The GIPR was a 'guaranteed' railway, which meant that it was constructed and operated by a private UK company, the share capital of which was underwritten by the Indian Government. All of the eight major railway lines of the time were thus supported.

The GIPR opened its first 20-mile section from Bombay to Tannah in 1853, only twenty years after the first railway was opened from Stockton to Darlington. Beyond this point the engineers were faced with the Western Ghats, a major escarpment bounding the western edge of the Deccan Plateau. There was much debate about which route to follow and

8. Letterhead showing the Albion Works site at which Harper & Co. were located from 1879, looking north, with the wind apparent from the west. The GNSR line from Waterloo to Kittybrewster can be seen in the foreground. The small figure in the lower right illustrates the Hadden Street (New Market Buildings) premises. The reference in the lower left to HM Royal Patent, granted in 1863, also serves to date the image.

one engineer even proposed that all Indian railways should be suspended throughout their course to avoid the animals! That would have provided Harper & Co. with a major business opportunity! Eventually one branch went north-east to join the East Indian Railway (which crossed the northern plain between Calcutta and Delhi) at Jabalpur. A second branch headed due east to Nagpur, the capital of the central provinces. Beyond this point there was a local narrow gauge railway to the rich agricultural area of Chhattisgarh. The later Nagpur Extension replaced the narrow gauge railway and extended the line from this area right across towards the east coast, joining the coastal railway from Madras to Calcutta, near the latter. This route was about 350 miles (322km), although not all of it was necessarily continuously fenced. Harpers, founded only in 1856, succeeded in contracting for the fencing of the Nagpur extension and perhaps for other sections. The cast posts with integral strainers were founded at the Mealmarket Street works from around 1860 and shipped by sea from Aberdeen. This and other Indian contracts underpinned the Harpers' business for many years, together with similar work at home for the developing GNSR railway system. The contract was described later as an 'enormous piece of work (that) not only brought John Harper much profit but much credit'.[4]

Harper & Co. thrived in the 1860s and 1870s and in 1879 the company moved to larger premises at Albion Street. These premises were strategically placed next to the GNSR Waterloo to Kittybrewster line; one wall of the foundry can still be seen today from the Beach Boulevard's bridge over the railway, looking south. This change in location resulted in a further development in the company's business, this time into components for power-driven machinery for the city's textile, grain and paper mills.

Harper & Co.'s functions at the Albion Iron Works were described in the Aberdeen Street Directory of 1881 as those of general founders, engineers, millwrights, blacksmiths and storemen. Specifically, this included making shafts of iron or steel, as well as the manufacture of couplings, pedestals and fixings, pulleys for belts and ropes, gear wheels, iron or mortice keyseaters for slotting the inside radius of wheels and pulleys of any diameter, and steel wire suspension bridges for foot traffic (described in promotional material as 'light, elegant and at small cost'). Interestingly, wire manufacture is no longer mentioned and the company may have sourced this elsewhere. Harpers also manufactured other products for home and foreign engineers who lacked production facilities. It had considerable success with its 'keyseater'. This machine was designed to make the grooves in the axle and the inner surface of a wheel to allow a key to be driven through both to lock the two together. The technique represented an advantage over the 'slotters' that were in use at that time by being applicable to wheels of any diameter. In addition, the keyways could be tapered slightly to provide added security for the driven key. This innovative device was manufactured and delivered to foundries elsewhere in Aberdeen and throughout the UK, but there is no evidence of any application for a patent.

Harper & Co. in mid-century was one of five major foundries in Aberdeen; these included the works of James Abernethy and Co., William Mackinnon & Co., Blaikie Bros and J.M. Henderson. All of these were iron founders, but each had its own particular niche. Abernethy was noted for the manufacture of ships' boilers and truss railway bridges and Mackinnon for the supply of commodity handling equipment for the plantations of the Empire. Blaikie is a name found in pavement fittings throughout the UK and Henderson cranes were involved in the building of both the rail and road bridges over the Firth of Forth. Against the background of this flourishing activity, Harper & Co., from its modest start as a worker of wire, developed rapidly both at home and abroad on the back of agricultural enclosure and railway expansion. As his company flourished, John Harper, entrepreneur and innovator, spotted a gap in the market for a new product, a light foot 'suspension' bridge. We now know something of his background, but how did his new idea take shape?

3

CHAIN AND ANCHOR

There is no reasonable doubt that in some extraordinary case this kind of bridge will be extended to one thousand feet once the subject shall be fully understood and should it ever be necessary.

(James Finley, 1809)

What exactly is a suspension bridge? Who first built them? And how had they developed before John Harper first started 'throwing' bridges across rivers, railways and ravines? These are some of the questions that require to be addressed now.

Foot suspension bridges were known to the ancients of China and India, according to Robert Stevenson, civil engineer and grandfather of the famous author R.L. Stevenson, in his Edinburgh *Philosophical Journal* article of 1821.[15] They were reputed to be of considerable length – one in Hindustan spanned 600ft (or 182.88m) – and their decks were laid directly on the main cables. Those described in the eastern Himalaya often had cables of bamboo or cane, which was stronger than hemp. They were of two types. The first was known as the 'Chinese' and consisted of two or more chains, tensioned by spar winches, on which a notched yoke sat with the passenger suspended below. The second type was the 'Tibetan', more akin to the modern suspension bridge, which featured a deck suspended from separate cables.[16] An early suspension bridge in the UK, the Winch chain bridge, with a 60ft (18.29m) span, was built over the River Tees in England for use by local miners. The deck lay directly on the main cables, which were fixed to both sides of the ravine, and was supplemented by handrails. Such bridges are referred to as *primitive* suspension bridges, by Tadaki Kawada, the noted Japanese civil engineer and academic,[17] today by the Nepalese as *suspended* bridges and by others

as *trail* bridges. Modern suspension bridges are different in design. In a modern suspension bridge, the deck is suspended from the main cables by means of vertical suspender rods or wires. The illustration shows this form and describes some of the bridge terms and synonyms used in this book.

This might be the time to introduce another bridge type which is sometimes wrongly described as a suspension bridge. A cable-stayed bridge is illustrated. Here, paired cables extend from the masthead to fixed points on the deck at increasing distances from the mast – there is no main cable. Thus each section of platform is normally supported by one or other mast pair. This contrasts with the suspension bridge, in which any section of deck is supported by all four masts of the bridge through its dependence upon the main cables.

The first suspension bridge of modern times, as defined above, was built at Jacob's Creek, Pennsylvania, by James Finley in 1801. It had a span of 70ft (21.34m) and measured 10ft 6in (3.20m) in width. Finley had been born in Ireland in 1856 and had emigrated to the USA as a boy. He later became a judge in Fayette, Pennsylvania, as well as building and distributing suspension bridges. He patented his suspension bridges and many were built by others under licence in the early years of the nineteenth century. Finley's cables were of chain, 'the chains must be allowed a sinking or curvature of nearly one sixth the span; and when this proportion is adhered to, the strength will be the same whether extended

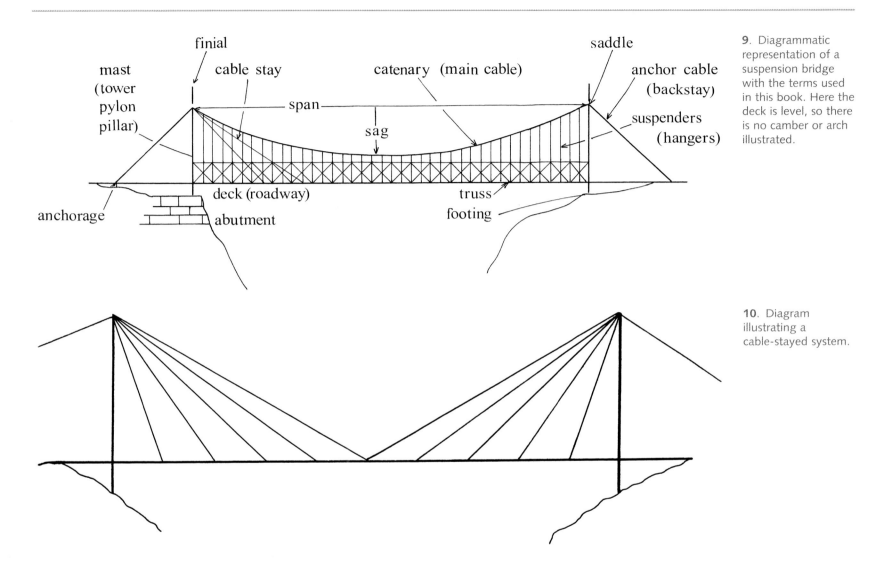

finial

saddle

mast
(tower
pylon
pillar)

cable stay

catenary (main cable)

anchor cable
(backstay)

span

suspenders
(hangers)

sag

deck (roadway)

truss

anchorage

footing

abutment

9. Diagrammatic representation of a suspension bridge with the terms used in this book. Here the deck is level, so there is no camber or arch illustrated.

10. Diagram illustrating a cable-stayed system.

to three feet or three hundred feet...' (Finley, Judge James, *A description of the Chain Bridge* (Uniontown, PA 1809) quoted by Sayenga).[18]

The next critical date in suspension bridge history is 1816, when Josiah White and Erskine Hazard, wire drawers selling wire to the local textile industry, built a light wire suspension over the Schuylkill River in Pennsylvania in order to allow their men to reach the company works.

The main cables on their bridge were comprised of three wires on each side, measuring (9.5mm) in diameter, probably running parallel to one another, over a span of 408ft (124.36m). This may have been the first foot suspension bridge to use wire cable and it may have been intended to be temporary, as a nearby chain bridge was being repaired. In the USA, the chain bridge held sway until the advent of the Fairmont Bridge in

Philadelphia, built with wire cables by Charles Ellet in 1842. By this time the German-born engineer Johan August (John Augustus) Roebling had arrived on the scene and virtually all suspension bridges in the USA thereafter were supported by wire cables, usually of iron, until Roebling's Brooklyn Bridge, completed in 1883, in which steel wire was used. (John Roebling also built the Ohio River bridge (1866) at Cincinnati where he used wire from Manchester – possibly steel wire.)

The main cable of a suspension bridge is often referred to as the 'catenary'. In physics and geometry, a catenary is the curve that a chain or cable assumes when only its ends are supported and it lies under its own weight. In a bridge the situation is complicated by the attachment of suspenders at equal distances (measured along the curve of the cable),

which, in turn, carry the weight of the deck and anything passing over it. Technically, the curve is no longer a catenary because it is distorted by the suspenders, but it very closely approximates one. In other situations the suspenders are spaced equally along the horizontal, the pattern most closely resembling a suspension bridge. The curve of the main cable is then most accurately described as a parabola. However, I shall follow the example of other authors by simply designating that part of the main cable between the tops of the towers or masts as the catenary, however it is disposed.

Later in the same year, 1816, Richard Lees, the owner of a textile mill in Galashiels, 'conceived of the idea of forming a foot-bridge, of slender iron wires, for the convenience of communicating readily with the different parts of his works'.[15] Galashiels was a prosperous Borders mill town at

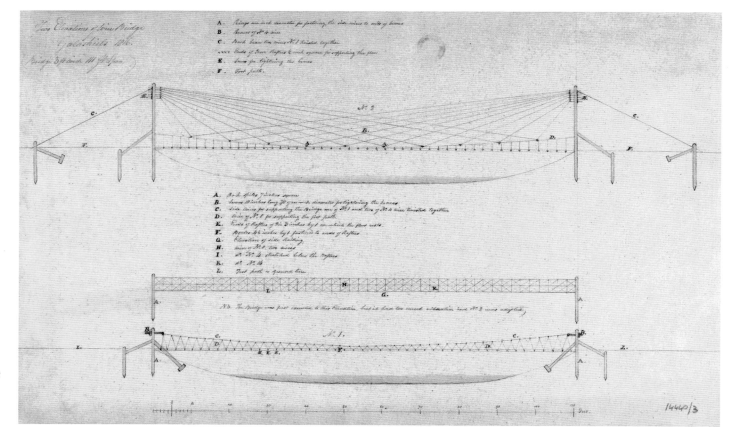

11. Lees' first bridge over the Gala Water, Galashiels, 1816. (*Scottish Record Office, courtesy of the Duke of Buccleuch and Keeper of the Records of Scotland*)

the confluence of the Gala Water and the River Tweed. Lees owned the Galabank Mill, which lay a little upstream of the town on the left bank of the Gala Water, but his only option for expansion was to acquire a mill on the opposite right bank. Workers who needed to travel between the mills had to make a detour to the centre of the town, where they were able to cross the river over a stone bridge; this could be avoided by the provision of a footbridge. The Gala is a rapid river that is often in spate and a clear spanned suspension bridge was the best option. Lees was aware of the American experience in Pennsylvania, which had been reported in the Edinburgh press,[19] and built the bridge with the assistance of Messrs Bathgate, a local millwright and a Thomas Mercer and Joshua Wood. Two drawings of the first Gala bridge survive. The first drawing (lower) shows a low-profile catenary slung from masts of only 5ft (1.52m) in height, with a span of 111ft (33.83m) and a deck supported by vertical suspenders. The cost of this first version was £40. The second drawing (upper) shows much taller masts of 18ft (5.49m) that subtend a number of paired 'stays' out to increasingly distant points on the catenary in a pattern that allows them to overlap with their opposite numbers. Thus the catenaries became mere intermediaries between the inclined stays and the deck. For this reason, Peters[20] and Ruddock[19] classify the bridge as cable-stayed, with the catenaries performing a secondary role. However, any section of deck still owed its stability to all four masts through the catenary, so, I submit, the essential feature is the catenaries and it remains a suspension bridge! Presumably the earlier version was too mobile for comfort. The wire catenaries at Galashiels were composed of three iron wires twisted together, as in spun thread, a technique not used in the other early bridges. The *Kelso Mail* reported:

> A wire bridge for foot passengers after the model of those constructed in America has just been erected across the Gala at Galashiels, and is found to answer the purpose exceedingly well and to every appearance may last for a number of years at little or no expense. The span, which is 111 feet, and the breadth 3 feet, makes it very neat and light in appearance, though with safety 20 or 30 people may be upon it at any one time. The whole expense of the little bridge is only £40. The public is very much indebted to the well-known spirit of Mr Lees for this useful introduction into the neighbourhood.[21]

Lees' bridge lasted until 1839, when it was swept away by the river in spate. Shortly afterwards, Richard Lees commissioned a new bridge to be built a little downstream. An amusing tale is told of this second bridge over the Gala Water:

> On one occasion a party of fishers were leistering salmon by torchlight, and a number of villagers congregated on the bridge in order to witness the sport. At length the fishers passed under the bridge, when its occupants changed their position to the other side, and, the chain at that side proving too weak, it broke, and the spectators were capsized into the water. Not much damage was done. One old woman, named Bet Watson, who had been enjoying her smoke, was heard informing some sympathisers that 'she didna care a bawbee for the tummel, if she hadna broken her cuttie (clay pipe)'.[22]

This second Lees bridge lasted until 1846, when it too was swept away. This is the last recorded wire suspension bridge in the UK until John Harper reintroduced them around 1870.

John Stevenson Brown, of the Edinburgh engineers Redpath & Brown, having examined Lees' effort at Galashiels, designed a wire footbridge to be erected across the River Tweed at King's Meadows near Peebles in the following year, 1817. Brown's design used only wire stays (No. 1 wire – 0.3in; 1.0cm) emanating from cast iron posts and no catenary. This was a cable-stayed bridge, probably the first in the UK, and not a suspension bridge.

Two other wire bridges are known to have been built before 1820, at, respectively, Thirlstane in the Scottish Borders and Garscube near Glasgow. No details of either survive.

Meanwhile, in 1817 the brothers John and Thomas Smith, builders and architects of Darnock, near Melrose, were asked by the Earl of Buchan to build a bridge at Dryburgh on the River Tweed. This was not to be a wire bridge but one of linked wrought iron bars – a chain bridge. Why did the Smith brothers choose to use wrought iron bars rather than wire? Chains had been used in the USA following James Finley's 1801 construction of a bridge in Pennsylvania, and had demonstrated currency for strength and stability. Wrought iron chains were either made to completion at the foundry or, usually, fabricated 'cold' on site, that is, without welding.

12. Lees' second bridge over the Gala Water 1839–1846, from a detail of an etching by an unknown artist dated 1845 of a view of Galashiels, the frontispiece of *The History of Galashiels* (Robert Hall, 1898, *National Library of Scotland*). Some cable stays are evident, but a catenary cannot be confirmed in this etching. The deck appears to be arched.

13. J.S. Brown's bridge over the River Tweed at King's Meadows, Peebles, 1817. *(National Library of Scotland)*

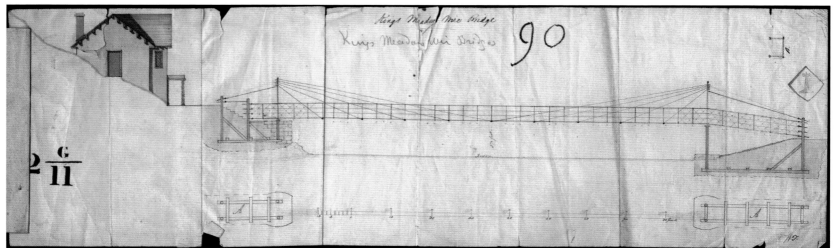

The Smith brothers' bridge at Dryburgh used four pairs of chain cable stays, which ran from timber end frames (masts and transom) to the deck. It also incorporated four under-deck chains of the same material. At one end of each bar was a closed eye, and at the other end, a hook or open eye that passed through its neighbour. The hook was then closed by hammering and its position maintained by a collar. The bridge was completed in August 1817 but five months later it was destroyed in a storm. As John Smith bemoaned in an entry in his journal, it was clear that the open links had failed, '…the work of half a year, demolished in an hour' (John Smith's diary, quoted by Ruddock).[19]

However, within a few months, John Smith had a proposal for a replacement bridge at Dryburgh. Samuel Brown and Thomas Telford, leading engineers of the day, may have visited the site to learn of the failure and no doubt discussed the new proposal. Both Telford and Brown were developing ideas about much larger suspension bridges at the time. Several authors ascribe the design and the construction of the second Dryburgh bridge to Samuel Brown, but Ruddock assures us that primary sources indicate otherwise.[19]

In 1818 the replacement footbridge, this time a foot suspension bridge, was completed. John Smith's design used paired catenary chains made up of wrought iron bars with intermediate welded links patented by Samuel Brown. The deck, supported also by chains, was strengthened with truss parapets, which much reduced the vertical motion of the bridge. It had a width of 4ft 6in (1.37m) at mid-span and lasted for thirty years. Its replacement of 1872 is still in use today.

Captain Samuel Brown had pioneered the development of wrought iron anchor chains and rigging during his naval career. On retiring from the Service, he set up his own iron works at Millwall in London and in 1817 patented the manufacture of flat eye bar links intended to replace the round and square chain rods then in use. Brown's naval background led him to prefer chains and he didn't think much of the idea of iron wire cable. In particular, Brown considered that water ingress would result in the deterioration of the vast surface area of the multiple wires. He had identified a flaw that still has resonance for today's suspension bridge builders.

Samuel Brown's greatest bridge was the first in the UK (and the first outside the USA) to carry vehicular traffic, as indeed it still does. The

15. The Union Bridge over the River Tweed today, looking north. In 1903, single catenary steel wire cables were added in case of failure of the chains.

14. An example of the flat wrought iron bar linked chain, with deck suspenders slung from the short links. The building in the centre background was previously the offices of James Abernethy & Co., Aberdeen.

Union Bridge that crosses the River Tweed at Paxton near Berwick, and uniting Scotland with England, was opened in 1820. Its construction depended on twelve main chains, but Captain Brown had chosen to eschew the use of supplementary stays, preferring to return to the 'purity' of James Finley's combination of a heavy catenary and rigid deck to give sufficient stiffness to allow the passage of heavier carts and coaches. Brown went on to build the Trinity Pier at Newhaven on the Firth of Forth, the Brighton Pier of 1822, a bridge over the River South Esk in 1829 at Montrose (which collapsed the following year), and the Wellington Bridge over the River Dee in Aberdeen. The Wellington Bridge survives, although it is closed to vehicles.

John Smith, who, with his brother Thomas, had constructed the first and second Dryburgh bridges, also designed and built a foot suspension bridge over the River Tweed at Gattonside, on the opposite bank to Melrose, although John Stevenson Brown's firm of Redpath & Brown was also involved. The Gattonside bridge opened in 1826. Here, stone towers supported the catenaries, which consisted of twin chains of wrought iron. Overall, its construction was similar to that of the bridge at Dryburgh. The bridge was refurbished in 1928 and again, more controversially, in 1992.[19]

Further north in Dundee, the Justice family, styled as ironmongers, built several light chain bridges in the Angus Glens, mostly between 1824 and 1834. These were entirely cable-stayed and without catenaries (although the bridge over the River Dee at Crathie acquired catenaries later when refurbished by Blaikie Bros of Aberdeen). Light, round, linked bars were used. By this time, all contemporary suspension bridge building in the UK used the chain-based design. James Dredge, of Bath, built the General's Well Bridge at Inverness (1854), the Victoria Bridge at Bridge of Oich (1850), and a further bridge over the River Clyde at Blantyre.

No summary of early nineteenth century suspension bridge building in the UK would be complete without reference to Scots engineer Thomas Telford's great suspension road bridge built to connect the town of Menai on the Isle of Anglesey with the North Wales mainland (1819–26). Incredibly, Telford's design was approved only two years after the completion of Lees' innovative footbridge at Galashiels. The early stages of the project featured collaboration between Samuel Brown and Telford, and Telford incorporated Brown's patent flat bar link chains.

The main span of the great Menai suspension bridge measures 580ft (176.78m) and comprises four sets of four flat-sectioned chains that dip 43ft (13.11m) from the horizontal (the sag). It carried two vehicular carriageways. Telford concentrated on the quality of the chains, each of which was loaded to twice its required tension and then struck with a hammer to reveal any flaw. The chains proved their worth in the storms that were to come when the deck suffered repeated damage, possibly as a result of inadequate stiffening.

In large bridges the problem of potentially self-destructive oscillation was addressed by increasing the weight of the chains. Charles Drewry, reviewing the progress of suspension bridge development in 1832, encapsulated the problem thus:

> …in suspension bridges of large dimensions, and consequently of great weight, the force that the suspended mass will acquire by being put in motion, increases rapidly… Therefore, when it becomes necessary to make the chains of a bridge

16. The Menai suspension bridge.

so heavy that vibration would be dangerous, it is advisable boldly to increase their weight, rather than to attempt to diminish it, and to bind and connect the several chains and the roadway firmly together, in order that there may be sufficient *mass* and *stiffness* in the bridge to *resist* motion, rather than yield to it readily.[23]

Telford's design, with its heavy chain catenary and rigid trussed decks, partly resolved the oscillation that occurred as something crossed the bridge. However, the bridge's residual mobility was subject to the exploits of another element: the wind. Wind can be random in force and direction, and the deck of a suspension bridge in adverse conditions can represent an aerofoil that leads to the bridge's destruction, such as occurred in the spectacular failure of the Tacoma Narrows Bridge in Puget Sound in Washington State in 1940. Not until the advent of the Severn and Forth Road bridges in the 1960s was this problem at least partly resolved.

The early part of the nineteenth century saw an interesting divergence in suspension bridge design between Great Britain on the one hand, and France and the USA on the other. In Great Britain, after the wire bridges of Richard Lees (Gala) and John and Thomas Smith (Peebles), chain bridges became universal, whereas in France and the USA the multi-strand wire cable bridge held sway. French Government engineers, notably Claude Navier, had visited the UK in 1821 and submitted a report to the French Government in 1823, favouring chain bridge construction. However, by the time the Seguin brothers of Annonay in the Ardeche were invited to design a bridge at Tournon in the Rhône Valley in 1824, they had already built a prototype 72ft (21.95m) bridge of wire, which confirmed their views on the use of wire and served as the basis of their plan for a bridge at Tournon-Tain. The significant new idea, borne of the local rope-making industry, was that 100 strands of very fine wire could be parallel-bundled to form catenary cables. Navier took some persuading, but eventually the Seguin brothers won the day and the contract was awarded for a double-span bridge, each span of which measured 280ft (85.34m). Navier went on to build a massive chain suspension bridge across the Seine at Pont des Invalides in Paris, which failed because of shortcomings in its foundations and anchorages.

The Seguin brothers also proposed a foot suspension bridge for access to the city of Geneva across the old ramparts, a bridge that was finally built by Guillaume Henri Dufour. Dufour (1787–1875) was a prominent politician who was responsible for establishing Switzerland's state of armed neutrality and chaired the conference that established the International Red Cross, as well as being an engineer. His was a wire cable bridge – Peters suggests that it was the first such construction in the world, dismissing Lees' effort at Galashiels as a 'temporary' structure.[20] As the bridge over the Gala Water lasted twenty-two years, it can hardly be seen as temporary. And what of the bridge built by Hazard and White over the Schuylkill River in Pennsylvania earlier in 1816? Again, Peters dismisses this as temporary, albeit with better reason. Certainly Dufour's bridge of 1823 at Geneva was very much more sophisticated than the earlier bridges, but then so was the Telford's Menai Bridge, under construction at the time.

Multi-wire cables had to be prefabricated at a site close to that of the bridge construction and required some allowance for their acute curvature over the saddles. They were then hoisted onto the saddles atop the towers. The next significant stage in the advancement of technology concerned the 'spinning' invention of Louise-Joseph Vicat. Vicat was an assistant engineer in the Corrèze district in south-central France, who had carried out research on cement mortars, particularly on underwater applications. He described his method as follows:

> When the piers, towers and abutments of a suspension bridge are finished, and the anchorages ready to receive the cables, let us suppose that a series of double wires, forming loops and all of equal length, have been prepared in advance in various rolls and wound one after the other on reeling machines. These wires are passed from one tower to the other with the help of a light endless rope, stretched like a flying fox, and moved like a chain pump. This job will be done more quickly than a man would take to run along the same line on level ground… We will limit ourselves to what seems most simple, a series of independent revolutions placed in superimposed layers on circular grooves at the anchorages, each layer containing an even number of wires. (Vicat, quoted by Pendet.)[24]

These revolutions or loops can be composed of two, four, six, etc., wires. More sophisticated 'spinners' could carry many more loops and heavier cables could be fabricated *in situ*. This technique was developed into a fully mechanised form by Washington Roebling in the Brooklyn Bridge (1883) and is now standard. The French went on to build a great many wire cable suspension bridges in Europe, far in excess of numbers in either the UK or USA. However, this wave of construction largely came to an end in 1850 when a pre-opening load test using a platoon of French soldiers went horribly wrong, with substantial loss of life.[25]

Although chain bridge construction continued after 1834, the utility of these bridges was increasingly limited by the dawn of the age of the railway. Few suspension bridges have been built for rail traffic. One of these, built by Samuel Brown in 1853, spanned the River Tees on the Stockton to Darlington railway. E.W. Serrell[26] described the scene:

> The only bridge known to the public, built upon the suspension principle, that has had locomotive trains upon it, was on the line of the Stockton and Darlington Railway in England. This bridge had been built for common road travel, but being in a good position to be used by the railway company, the track was laid on it, and a trial made. Mr Stephenson stated that the entire structure rose up 3 feet before the locomotive at ordinary speed; and that the entire work was nearly destroyed by the passage of the train. Piles were driven into the bed of the river, and the roadway secured to them. Still the structure was useless, as the pile were alternately drawn out and driven in by the action of the chains and the loads on the track.

More successful was the railway bridge at Niagara Falls, built by John Roebling in 1855. This was a truss-decked bridge that carried a railway above and a roadway below. The decks were connected by side trusses so that the railway formed the upper and the roadway the lower inner surfaces of a box.

This chapter summarises briefly, and somewhat selectively, the state of the art of suspension bridge building in the first half of the nineteenth century, with particular reference to the UK. It sets the scene for the latter half of the century, when few suspension bridges were built for major highways in the UK and the pace of suspension bridge construction slowed, even in France and the USA. However, this period saw the establishment of the country estate and of developing Empire. This created a niche market for the re-establishment of the light wire foot suspension bridge, which is ideal for out-of-the-way places at home and abroad.

4

SUSPENSION, TENSION AND ARCH

You see, he knew how to tension wire.
(Louis R. Harper, 1902–73)

So said my father to me many years ago, referring to his grandfather John, and I've never forgotten the essential catalyst that allowed the local fencer to become an international bridge builder. In this chapter we will trace the evolution of the Harper light wire suspension bridge. By 1850, as we learned in Chapter 3, several notable suspension bridges had been constructed in the UK, usually employing chain and having rigid decks capable of taking cart traffic. By that time, few, if any, manufacturers were making wire suspension bridges in the UK.

Was John Harper aware of the developments in the USA and France? Certainly he would have known of the Scottish chain suspension bridges, the so-called blacksmith bridges, particularly in the Scottish Borders. After all, as a young fencer in Edinburgh and Glasgow he would have ranged far and wide in the estates and farms of the Borders and Midland Valley. Whether he read Stevenson's account[15] of the endeavours of Finley, Lees and Smith and their early bridges which were mostly gone before he was born, is doubtful. British engineer Charles Drewry's treatise of 1832, describing suspension bridges in Great Britain, the USA and France, together with the associated mathematics, might have been more accessible[27]. On the other hand he was probably a subscriber to *The Engineer*, the foremost periodical of the time, which would have carried news and debate about bridges of all kinds. John Harper knew how to tension wire and knew that his fence wire strainer could be used

for applications other than fencing, such as for telegraph wires, and, 'for straining wires in any case in which they are extended and supported by means of a series of pillars or posts',[10] although, in his patent submission, dated 1863, he did not mention suspension bridges, even as a possibility. It is more likely that his approach to bridges was incremental and empirical. Starting with his knowledge and experience of straining wire, he 'grew' the fencing concept into one that applied to the construction of suspension bridges on a basis of trial and error, or experimentation, rather than one of calculation – although that came later.

The chain suspension bridges of such as Samuel Brown and certainly Telford were major and expensive undertakings. They were designed to carry major roads and often had two carriageways. Clearly, there was a market at home and later, throughout the developing world for a lighter, cheaper construction for foot traffic. J.R. Hume, writing in 1977 of light Scottish suspension bridges, commented, 'It is possible, though improbable, that the bridges of this type were first used in the North of Scotland'[28], without adducing evidence either in favour of the possibility or its improbability. A footbridge that could be used on country estates, thrown across a Himalayan gorge or erected to allow passengers access to the opposite platform at a new railway station found a market. Materials could be minimal and cheap, and construction was fast – we shall discover in Chapter 5 that John Harper's bridges usually took about two weeks to erect. Steel wire rope, with its economy and strength, was his answer, supported by timber masts with timber decks, both sourced locally. This was dependent on whether the wire could be efficiently tensioned between 'dead' anchorages, and periodically re-tensioned in the event that it was extended by load or temperature. Thus the only parts to be manufactured for dispatch would have been a set of tensioners, the main, deck and anchor cables and the suspender rods. This was a speedy and economical way to build a bridge. Furthermore, the light construction of this type of bridge suited an Aberdeen foundry located some distance from both the sources of its raw materials and major markets.

We have seen that after a brief period of using iron wire, early nineteenth century bridge builders in the UK opted to use heavy chain, stretching from massive towers and suspending rigid trussed decks that were able to carry heavy loads over wide spans with minimal movement. The Harper bridges were not of this genre. They were light foot suspension bridges, designed for erection in out-of-the-way places, and made of components that could be transported along footpaths by man or animal. Hence, reducing deck movement by the use of heavy chains and steel deck trusses was not an option, although Harper & Co.'s Mealmarket Street foundry would have been capable of producing cast iron bar links.

John Harper's starting point was Lees' bridges over the Gala Water – this was light and cheap but unfortunately highly mobile. How could a light bridge be made rigid? All of the early Harper bridges had two unique features – a particular form of suspension and the cable tensioner.

A NEW SYSTEM OF SUSPENSION

Not for nothing are light foot suspension bridges often known as 'swing bridges' or 'shakin' briggies' – to the dismay of the adult and delight of the child in equal measure. They were very lively to cross, especially by people walking in groups – soldiers, for example, were required to break step for fear of instigating an uncontrollable oscillation of the deck.[25] [27] These light bridges had to acquire stiffness by means other than the weight of their cables and decks.

John Harper addressed the problem of the lack of stiffness by matching his lightweight steel wire rope catenary with a cable of the opposite curvature. This technique was first seen in Isle de Bourbon (now Réunion) in the Indian Ocean, where Marc Brunel (father of Isambard Kingdom Brunel) built a bridge in January 1823.[27] Brunel's chain bridge

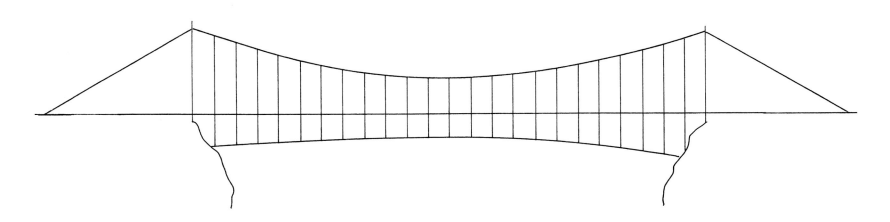

17. Diagram of Marc Brunel's bridge showing a level and rigid deck and a subdeck cable of the opposite curvature in a design intended to allow the bridge to withstand wind.

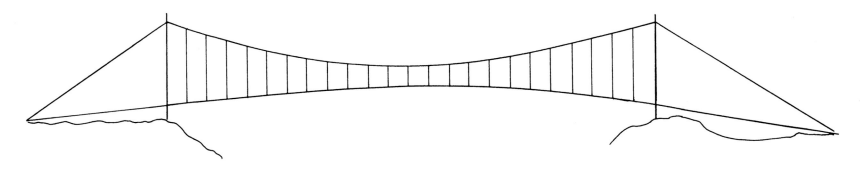

18. John Harper's system of suspension using cables with opposite curvatures to enhance stiffness. The dip of the main or catenary cables is the 'sag' and the rise or arch of the deck is called the 'camber'.

was built in Sheffield, dismantled and shipped out to Isle de Bourbon. To counteract the winds of the region, it was stayed by cables anchored at either side to the cliff below the abutments, rising to just beneath the deck at mid-span. Vertical rods linking each to the deck above were counteracted by the suspenders connecting the catenary with the deck. A similar system with convex cables below the bridge was used in bridges over the Colorado (1928) and Arkansas (1929) rivers in the USA. The only other record of construction using this system of suspension refers to a multispan bridge with pretensioned cables at deck level, erected at San Marcos, El Salvador, in 1952.[19]

In the case of the Harper bridges, the cable of opposite curvature to the steel wire rope catenary also served to support the deck and was anchored either to the foot of the masts or to the main anchorage. This was an innovative and elegant solution by John Harper to the problem of mobility in bridges such as these with unstiffened decks.

The Harper 'opposed curves' continue to define the suspension bridge to this day in Nepal, over 100 years later. In the mid-nineteenth century, this represented a bold and visionary design[13]. The arrangement was to remain basic to all Harper bridges for the next thirty years until 1900, when Louis would collaborate with James Abernethy & Co., Aberdeen (see Chapter 6). It is not known whether John knew of Brunel's design,

whether he had derived the idea from descriptions in Drewry's book[27], whether he had come across the principle elsewhere, or whether his adoption of this technique was simply empirical. I favour the latter because all evidence shows that the arrangement of the Harper bridge at deck level was unique at the time.

Professor Colin O'Connor of Brisbane[29], an authority on Australia's early bridges, pointed out that with this system of suspension, the deck shape must first be raised at mid-span so that the stiffness of the completed structure can be enhanced. The photograph of the Narva bridge, erected in 1908 in Estonia, shows that the first suspender linking the catenary to the deck cables is at mid-span. Louis Harper supplied suspenders tooled to an accuracy of $\frac{1}{16}$in (1.6mm) in order to preform an arch designed to ensure that the relationship between the catenary and the opposing deck cable would establish the maximum degree of stiffness. The ratio of catenary sag below the point at which the catenary reached the mast to span was usually about 1:12; the ratio of the rise or camber to the span of the deck was usually about 1:50 (i.e. 1ft per 50ft of span).

In 1870, ensuring this degree of stiffness or relative rigidity in such a light structure by dint of the considerable tension applied at eight points to two pairs of cables curving towards one another was made possible by the Harpers' patented cable tensioner.

19. The first suspenders are placed at mid-span to create the arch or camber of the deck cable, as demonstrated in this photograph of the 1908 bridge over the River Narva, Estonia. (See also Figures 91 and 92) (*Aberdeen Art Gallery & Museums Collections*)

20. (a) John Harper's plan for the Ravenscraig bridge shows three in-mast tensioners at the terminations of all three cables. (*Aberdeen Art Gallery & Museums Collections*) **(b)** A cable tensioner on the far post of the Birkhall bridge, showing four keyways in the spindle and three in the casing, with a key inserted at 12 o'clock. (*T.M. Day*)

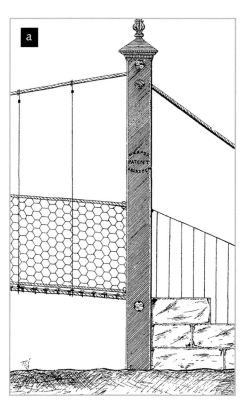

THE CABLE TENSIONER

We have heard how the fortunes of Harper & Co. as fencers were based on the 1863 patenting of the wire strainer and how a key was used to lock the spindle in position. Sometime after 1863 but before 1871, this concept was applied to create Harper bridges in two ways, using internal and external cable tensioners. The internal cable tensioner was very similar to the fence strainer, being held within a hollow cast post. The earliest known example was applied at the Ravenscraig bridge near Dundee in 1872. This used three tensioners per pillar to tension, respectively, the span, anchor and deck cables. Each tensioner had, like the fence strainer, four notches in the spindle and three on the casing. Thus, as the spindle was turned by its spanner, an opportunity to lock the two together with a single peg or key came at approximately every 30 degrees of rotation A similar bridge using this technique was built across the River Muick at Birkhall, Deeside in Aberdeenshire in 1880 and is still in use today. The spans of these two bridges were a modest 55ft (16.76m) and 60ft (18.29m), respectively.

Tensioning cable over a large span would have been a problem for such a small-scale device and thus, at about this time (1871 or earlier), there is evidence of the development of an external cable tensioner. This larger device was used, possibly for the first time, in the construction of a now ruined bridge spanning up to 100ft (30.48m) in Glen Tanar, Aberdeenshire. The tensioner shown in the illustration represents the earliest model of the external cable tensioner. Here, the tensioner is enclosed in a box attached to the timber mast. It measures 6.5in (16.25cm) wide and 6 × 6in (15.00 × 15.00cm) in cross-section. The cable passed through the mast into the open-backed box, where it was threaded through a fenestration in the spindle before being wound on. A spanner was applied to the nut on one side of the spindle, at the other side of which were four notches or keyways, each of which could be used to connect with any of the five keyways on the casing. As the spindle is turned, the single key can be inserted after a turn of 18 degrees from the previous position. This allowed for a considerable improvement in tension control compared with that afforded by the internal cable tensioners used at Ravenscraig and Birkhall.

21. The smaller external cable tensioner used at the Tanarmouth bridge (*c.* 1870) has four keyways in the spindle and five on the casing.

Further up Glen Tanar, there is evidence of the use of an even larger cable tensioner in a bridge of similar span. Here, the cable tensioner measured 9in (22.5cm) across and 12 × 12in (30.00 × 30.00cm) in cross-section. Examples of the two tensioners are shown in the illustrations. In the larger external tensioner, the spindle had six keyways and the casing eight. Thus, the spindle can turn 15 degrees between

22. Detail of a picture taken almost certainly in Glen Tanar around 1927, with an unmistakable Harper bridge in the background. *(Glentanar Estate)*

23. Comparison of the smaller, earlier, external cable tensioner (*c.* 1870) with the later larger one in **(a)** a frontal view, **(b)** the side elevation, where the four keyways in the cylinder and five in the casing of the smaller tensioner contrast with the six spindle keyways and eight casing keyways of the larger unit, and **(c)** an oblique rear view showing the fenestration in the spindles that would have received the end of the cable after its passage through the mast.

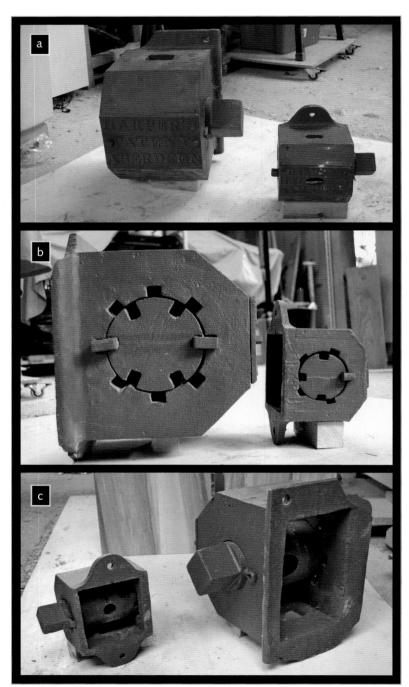

locking positions. This represents only a small advance on the smaller external tensioner but it has other advantages. In the larger tensioner, the design allows two keys to be inserted, conferring additional security, and the larger size allows more cable to be accommodated and greater mechanical advantage.

An examination of the devices shown above and in this illustration begs the question of just how much cable could be contained in the various external and internal tensioners. The answer is a few feet only. How then

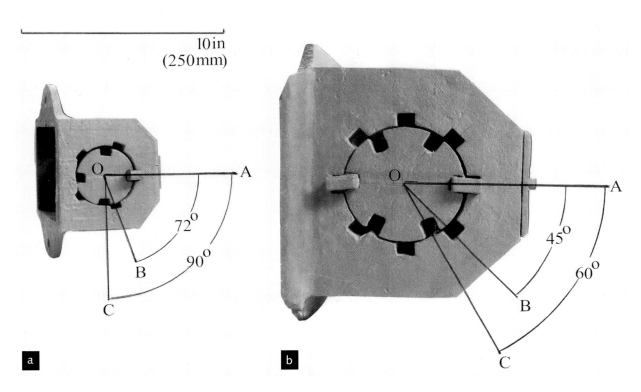

24. (a) In the smaller external tensioner, withdrawal of the key allows the spindle to move; the shortest distance possible is anticlockwise through the angle BOC (i.e. 90°−72°=18°). The movement can also be clockwise for the same distance. **(b)** In the larger tensioner, once both keys are withdrawn, the least distance the spindle can move is the angle BOC, which is 15°.

were these cables attached, given their weight, to the tops of the masts? It is likely that the cable was attached just a couple of feet from its end to a secondary, temporary system of tensioning such as a block and tackle. This would allow the loose end to be threaded through the mast and round the spindle of the tensioner. The spindle would then be turned to the correct tension and the secondary system detached. The final tension in those early bridges would most probably be decided by eye as the deck was applied.

The larger cable tensioner became the standard device used in all further bridges up to 1893, including that built over the Aberdeenshire River Dee at Waterside, Aboyne in 1871. The date of the latter bridge suggests that the bridge erected at Tanarmouth was an earlier construction and that it was probably erected between 1863 and 1871. It seems that around 1871 Harper & Co. was manufacturing these two very different designs of bridge using, respectively, internal and external tensioners, although both were based on the same fence strainer patent. At this time,

the manufacture of wheels, spindles (or axles) and keys represented a basic part of Harpers' mainstream business as a foundry supplying power-drive machinery to Aberdeen's numerous mills.

Initially, two cable tensioners were mounted on each mast – a tensioner mounted at the top of the mast was applied to the catenary, and another mounted near the foot was applied to the deck cable. The anchor cable was attached just below the upper tensioner by an eye bolt. Later, a third cable tensioner intended for the anchor cable replaced the eye bolt. The figure 25 shows the relationship of the cable tensioner to the posts. The cables are seen passing through the mast to the rear of their respective tensioners and crossing one another in mid-mast.

To span greater distances than, say, the Birkhall bridge (90ft; 27.43m), greater pylon height was required, for which larch, pine or other timbers were usually readily sourced from the landowner in question. The pylon height was derived from the span, the high water level and the state of the

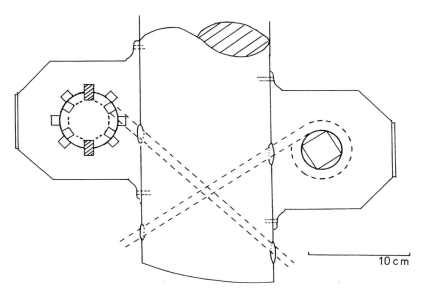

25. Side elevation of the cable tensioner *in situ*, showing the cables passing through the mast to reach the open rear of the cable tensioners.

route it took between anchorages, via the top of one pylon and over a saddle, then over the other pylon and down to the anchorage on the other side. The simplicity of the Harper arrangement accommodated the need to erect these bridges in remote areas, sometimes with very minimal engineering resources. A hefty spanner (25kg; 55lb) and a good head for heights were all that were required!

Over time, the design evolved. Firstly, the timber pylons of early bridges were often replaced with paired 'I-section' steel beams. The cable tensioners were reapplied and the bridge geometry remained pretty much unchanged. Louis Harper then introduced the use of conventional main cables over saddles, but retained the tensioners for the deck cables. After 1893, the bridge cable tensioner, which had represented the mainspring of the bridge business, was finally abandoned.

bank. Usually they were between 12ft (3.66m) and 20ft (6.10m) above the deck.

In these early bridges, the main cable was manufactured in three separate parts consisting of, respectively, the portion that would extend from the bank anchorage to the top of the pylon, the portion extending between the tops of the pylons and, finally, the portion extending from the top of the second pylon to the bank anchorage at the opposite end of the bridge. This required four pairs of tensioning boxes. Although rather basic, this arrangement had its advantages. Firstly, each section was relatively short and direct, and thus could be tensioned easily and precisely.

Secondly, the absence of a saddle at the mast top over which the cable would pass (see Figure 22) resulted in less frictional loss of tension. Thirdly, the use of individual components rather than a single cable running from anchorage to anchorage made erection and adjustment simpler and carriage to the site easier. In the bridges constructed by other engineers, tensioning of the main cable had to accommodate the indirect

26. The bridge at Feugh Lodge, near Banchory, Aberdeenshire, showing full conventional main cables. This was possibly the last bridge in which cable tensioners were used for the deck cables. (*University of Aberdeen George Washington Wilson Collection*)

27. The common anchorage as seen at Mangaltar, Nepal.

Louis Harper introduced cast iron tubular pylons in 1893. Bridges built with these pylons used full conventional bank-to-bank main cables attached to anchorages that also retained the deck cables: the 'common anchorage'.

The figure shows a common anchor holding both cables and including carrier blocks to which the cables were swaged and adjusting straining screws. By the mid-1890s, lattice steel pylons appeared for the first time at Keswick, on the Harper bridge built there over the River Greta. Once again, deck and suspension cables were led to common bank anchorages.

STEEL WIRE ROPE

Albeit that John Harper's bridges are defined by their system of suspension and the use of the cable tensioner, they are also characterised by another feature which, if not unique, was unusual and innovative – the use of steel rope. Steel wire rope was invented in 1834 by Wilhelm Albert (1787–1846), a German mining administrator, who noted metal fatigue in the chains then used in hoists within the Clausthal Caroline mine in the Hartz Mountains. Thereafter, Robert Stirling Newall (1812–1889),

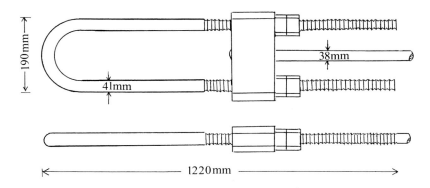

28. Detail from an original Louis Harper plan showing a main cable swaged into the block through which the limbs of the strainer adjusting screw pass. This in turn would be connected to the staple bolt embedded in the anchorage.

who established R.S. Newall & Co. in Gateshead, a firm that is as well known today as Turner & Newall, developed a machine for making wire rope, which he patented in 1840. Newall's rope had four strands with four wires to the strand. In the same year, 1840, John Roebling made his first use of wire rope, which he had brought into full production by 1848 at his Trenton, New Jersey factory. However, initially Roebling used wire from steelmaker Johnson & Nephew, Manchester for his Ohio Bridge at Cincinnati,[30] although it is not known whether this was steel wire. Seyenga[18] states that the first use of steel wire rope in the USA was in 1872, at Niagara Gorge. In Britain, the use of wire as a catenary had been unheard of since the iron wire catenaries and stays of the border bridges built before 1820, but after 1858, steel became much more readily available due to the introduction of the Bessemer process. In 1871, John Harper became among the first in Britain to use steel wire rope as a catenary. His example was followed by Sir John Fowler (1817–1898) in his bridge over the Corrieshalloch Gorge in Sutherland in 1874. Later exponents included Blaikie Bros of Aberdeen in their suspension bridge over the Aberdeenshire Dee at Abergeldie (1885), and William Bell, a local blacksmith who built a suspension bridge over the River Wharfe at Hebden, North Yorkshire in the same year. John Harper never used chain.

His background as a fencer and his fence tensioner led him directly to this new steel wire rope, which would facilitate the development of his system of suspension.

By 1930, the dawning age of the motor car implied that light suspension bridges for foot and cart traffic had served their purpose. Large rigid bridges, many made of reinforced concrete and box girders, allowed for satisfactory spans. However, in the 1930s and certainly since then, there has been a resurgence of interest in the suspension bridge. Its essential affordances of substantial span and low wind resistance, at relatively low cost, have resulted in the re-emergence of the suspension bridge as the optimal method of providing extended span. Examples include the Golden Gate Bridge in San Francisco (1937), the Forth Road Bridge in Scotland (1964) and the Severn Bridge between England and Wales (1966), to name but a few. Problems with corrosion within the multi-strand cables (predicted by Samuel Brown back in 1816) have been of concern and may explain the development of the rod and cable-stayed cantilever-style bridges. This type of bridge uses principles similar to those of the bridges built by Richard Lees at Galashiels (1816) and J.S. Brown at Peebles (1817) and seen today in the Kohlbrand Bridge at Hamburg (1974) and the Millau Viaduct in France (2004). However, for the longest spans, the suspension bridge continues to reign supreme. Prime examples include the Akashai Kaikyo Bridge in Japan (6,532ft; 199m) and the Storebaelt Bridge between Denmark and Sweden (5,328 feet, 1,624m).

THE RAVAGES OF TIME

In comparison with arched stone bridges, which are supported by compression, suspension bridges under tension are ephemeral structures. Many large country estates found themselves struggling through the economic ravages visited upon them by the twentieth century and the maintenance of footbridges became of low priority. Bridges in the public domain fared better. Of the timber-masted bridges, none remain, although remnants can occasionally be seen (at Tanarmouth in Aberdeenshire, Shocklach in Cheshire and Craighall in Tayside). The wooden masts usually lasted about fifty years. The bridge at Tanarmouth possibly represents the earliest Harper bridge of its kind to remain *in situ*, but it may have been re-sited and re-masted at some stage in the twentieth century.

The main cause of the failures of early bridges was flood. An examination of the remains of the Tanarmouth bridge suggests the mechanism for this failure.

As the river rose in spate, it would have engulfed the bridge with enormous power, pulling the deck downstream until the bridge gave way. The timber masts on the right bank were snapped at the level of the deck cables and tensioners, and the deck cable, with any remaining deck and its tensioners, was carried away. This seems to be confirmed by the presence of large longitudinal defects or slots in the lower end of the timber masts, which extend to the level at which the mast snapped off. These must represent the tearing out of the cable through the mast end.

This may indicate a flaw in the design of these early bridges, for although the main cable's tension was balanced by that of the anchor cable inserted at the same level, no balancing force was applied to the deck cable and thus the weakest point of the structure would have been the lower end of the mast. This, together with the self-evident fact that the spate would have engaged the deck first, probably accounts for the evidence found in the wreck of this bridge.

The later bridges built using cast iron masts, such as those at Sellack on the River Wye and Falkirk on the River Carron, fared better and the former is still in use, maintained by the local authority. Of the bridges with lattice masts, some fell into disrepair and had to be replaced or removed, but many were to suffer obsolescence that overtook the problems of their maintenance when pedestrian travel gave way to vehicular transport by road. At least four Harper lattice-masted bridges are still in use in Nepal and are well maintained, as are those at Newquay in Cornwall, Cambus o'May in Aberdeenshire and Aberlour, Banffshire.

This chapter has explored the principle features of the Harper foot suspension bridge, particularly John Harper's system of suspension, which may have been unique at the time. Now we turn to the bridges themselves and examine how John Harper's principles of suspension, tension and arch found expression.

5

FENCER TO BRIDGE BUILDER: THE BRIDGES OF JOHN HARPER

These bridges, light, airy and elegant as they appear in construction,
are really of great strength.

(*Aberdeen Daily Free Press*)

This chapter deals with the early bridges of John Harper, from the earliest known bridges of around 1870 to those constructed in 1889, when Louis left the company to set up on his own. The fence post patent specification did not include suspension bridges as a possible example of the application of the patent, so this suggests that the first bridge was after 1863. As we have seen, the systems of suspension in all of the early Harper bridges held two features in common – the catenary was tensioned against the arched deck and both cables were tensioned by the Harpers' patent wire strainer (see Figure 29). The sequence in which these early bridges will be described relates to the evolution of their design, rather than their strict chronology. The statistics of each bridge may be found in Appendix 1.

The bridge design that follows most naturally from the fencing work of Harper & Co. was first seen at an agricultural show, possibly in Banff in 1870. It could be described as a fencer's bridge, with low masts and in-post tensioners.

RAVENSCRAIG, DUNDEE, OVER THE CALEDONIAN RAILWAY

A press release issued at the time of the opening of the bridge at Birkhall (see below) referred to a bridge of similar design having been built for a Colonel Sandeman at Ravenscraig, near Dundee. We established contact with Ian McCraw, a distant descendant of Col Sandeman, who gave us some indication of where the Colonel's old house was likely to have been. The site of the mansion of Ravenscraig today is Ravenscraig Gardens, which lies off Broughty Ferry's Dundee Road. My wife and I explored the area with our grandchildren, but could find no feature that would justify the construction of even a small bridge. However, the land of Ravenscraig does extend down to the railway as it runs from Dundee to Broughty Ferry. Accompanied by our grandchildren, I scoured the ivy in the garden above a railway cutting, but failed to reveal any clues. A bridge from the property across the railway to access the foreshore could not be identified in local maps of around 1900. Ian McCraw then suggested that we might turn our attention to other possibilities involving the owner. Col Sandeman had owned the mill and also another residence at Stanley in Perthshire. Could he have sited a bridge there? The fine mill buildings are now being restored as a museum and housing. On a visit to the new museum in 2009, we admired a portrait of Col Sandeman with his two black labradors. It took me back to a time when I had two black labradors to walk every day … and led me to imagine the frustration of a well-to-do gentleman with two dogs, who was separated from the dog-walking paradise of the seashore at Broughty Ferry. Of course, the bridge had to have been built over the railway at his home at Ravenscraig!

Further searches at Aberdeen Museums identified a plan relating to a bridge at Dundee. Sandeman's bridge did indeed cross over the cutting at the foot of his ground at Ravenscraig, at exactly the spot our grandchildren had searched unsuccessfully for its remains. The *Courier & Argus* of Monday, 2 September 1872 provides some of the details of that day:

29. The basic early bridges of John Harper had two features in common that related to their system of suspension: the main or catenary cable was tensioned against the arched deck, and the main and deck cables were tensioned by the Harpers' patent wire strainer.

30. This type of bridge was marketed at agricultural shows. The date of this photograph is unknown, but as the bridge is identical to that at Birkhall, it was probably taken around 1870. *(Aberdeen Art Gallery & Museums Collections)*

31. John Harper's elevation of the bridge built near Dundee in 1872. *(Aberdeen Art Gallery & Museums Collections)*

PLAN OF
{Harper's Patent}
— WIRE SUSPENSION BRIDGE —
FOR
Colonel Sandeman
OF RAVENSCRAIG
WEST FERRY
DUNDEE

OPENING OF A WIRE BRIDGE AT RAVENSCRAIG

A fine bridge, which has been erected over the railway by Col. Sandeman at his residence at Ravenscraig, and which affords communication between the grounds and the beach of the river, was opened on Saturday afternoon by the Earl of Strathmore, immediately before the regatta. The bridge was constructed by Harper & Co. of Aberdeen and is a highly finished piece of workmanship. It is wholly of wire and supported on iron pillars, within which is the apparatus for working it. The span is fifty feet and the bridge is capable of bearing 7½ tons of people. The whole work of construction and fitting was executed in five days, at a cost of £80. When the Earl of Strathmore had walked over the bridge in order to assume his duties on board the Fairweather as Commodore, the fact was announced by a salute of nine guns being fired, and the band of the artillery Volunteers starting up an inspiriting air.

John Harper's drawing of 1872 shows a bridge suspended across a double-track railway as the latter passes through a cutting. The masts or pillars are about 10ft 6in (3.20m) high and the bridge span extends 55ft (16.76m). The main cables and the deck cables are tensioned by in-mast cable tensioners, but the design includes tensioners for the anchor cables. The drawing does not show any anchorages, but we can assume they are 'dead' (i.e. that any adjustment device would be located at the pillar). The deck is arched to give a rise of 1ft 3in (0.38m) and is tensioned against the catenary. The main and deck cables would have been made of steel rope. The deck, the *Courier & Argus* tells us, was wholly constructed of woven wire and the bridge used no timber in its construction. A similar bridge was erected for HRH the Prince of Wales, at Birkhall, on the Balmoral Estate, in 1880.

RIVER MUICK, AT BIRKHALL, ABERDEENSHIRE

My son Ross and I first visited the Birkhall bridge around 1985. We were allowed access to the Balmoral Estate and to the garden of Birkhall. Birkhall is situated on high ground to the north of the River Muick, a tributary of the River Dee that courses through Aberdeenshire, and is located a little distance below the Falls of Muick. The grounds stretch down to the river, which is crossed by the bridge. The local press reported:

WIRE BRIDGE AT BIRKHALL FOR THE PRINCE OF WALES

Messrs Harper & Co., Aberdeen, have just finished the erection of one of their wire suspension bridges over the river Muick at Birkhall for His Royal Highness the Prince of Wales. The bridge is 60 foot span, and is entirely constructed of steel wire, thoroughly galvanised. It has a platform or roadway of three and a half feet width – the sole not being of wood, as is commonly the case, but of finely woven netting, kept in its place both by tension, and by being supported by a diagonal framing between tightened ropes running from the cast iron columns at either side of the river. At the place where the new bridge crosses the Muick, nearly half a score of wooden bridges had been destroyed by ice, floods of wind during the last thirty years. The bridge, as usual, was erected under the superintendence of Mr John Harper, of Seafield, the patentee, whose experience enabled him, with the assistance of three men, to complete the structure within the comparative short space of a week, and a cost altogether of under £100. It is intended that several similar structures will be erected in the district – one of them possibly to take the place of the rope and cradle used for the crossing at Abergeldie. [This didn't, in fact, happen. A suspension bridge with a rigid deck was built across the River Dee at Abergeldie Castle, a little downstream of Balmoral, by Blaikie Bros., of Aberdeen, in 1885.]

Like the bridge at Ravenscraig, the bridge at Birkhall had low profile pylons, shown here to rise to a mere 8ft (2.44m) in height, and the main and deck cables were tensioned by the Harpers' patent within the hollow cast iron pylon (see Figure 33). This figure shows the Birkhall bridge today. Dr T.M. Day, formerly of Robert Gordon University, Aberdeen and an authority on bridge archaeology, has pointed out that the pillars were probably cast in three sections and fitted together on site. The tensioning device is similar in scale to the fence strainer, but includes a nut that protrudes at one side. The number of notches is the same as that on the fence post, so that they meet at 90-degree intervals on the rotating spindle and approximately 120-degree intervals on the casing, allowing insertion of the locking key. As with the Ravenscraig bridge, the deck was of woven wire so that the bridge was devoid of wood. The anchor cables are duplicated, but are attached to the mast by eye bolts, rather than by a tensioner as at Ravenscraig. Apparently the Birkhall bridge followed a succession of timber bridges, each of which were washed away by flood and ice flows. This more mobile suspension bridge has lasted since 1880,

32. The bridge at Birkhall on the Balmoral Estate, 1880. (*Aberdeen Art Gallery & Museums Collections*)

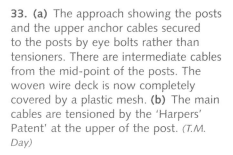

33. (a) The approach showing the posts and the upper anchor cables secured to the posts by eye bolts rather than tensioners. There are intermediate cables from the mid-point of the posts. The woven wire deck is now completely covered by a plastic mesh. (b) The main cables are tensioned by the 'Harpers' Patent' at the upper of the post. (*T.M. Day*)

and is still in use today. It is the sole remaining bridge designed and built by John Harper.

John Harper had expressed the hope that several more of these bridges might be erected in the district, but we have not uncovered any indications that they were. Cunliffe Brooks of Glentanar was keen on his Royal Deeside connections[31] – I wonder if the early bridge opposite Glentanar House was originally a stylish construction built after the pattern of that at Birkhall?

The wider the span, the taller the masts needed to be. Larger bridges generated greater tension and thus the winding gear – the cable tensioners – had to be scaled up to match. Masts were now generally constructed of local timber, usually larch, and the tensioners were contained within boxes that were externally applied to the masts on the opposite side from the span. The deck cables curved upward, being tensioned against the main cable. The anchor cables were initially attached to the masts by eye bolts, just below the main cable tensioner, but soon came to involve the use of tensioners placed opposite those of the main cables at the masthead. All of the Harper bridges built between around 1870 and 1887 followed this pattern, with the notable exception of John Harper's more sophisticated designs at Ravenscraig and Birkhall and displayed for marketing purposes at an agricultural show.

BRIDGES ON THE TANAR

In a letter to Aberdeen Town Council in September 1871, John Harper cited his experience of building bridges, 'similar to several Bridges which I have recently erected on the Dee and the Tanar on the Aboyne Estates for the Marquis of Huntly, and Mr Cunliffe Brooks, MP'. We are unsure of what he may have meant by 'several', and whether there were indeed several bridges over the Dee, over its tributary the Tanar, or over both in combination. We knew about the bridge over the Dee, west of Aboyne at Waterside but the only thing we knew about Glen Tanar was that Harper & Co. had fenced large parts of it. However, perusal of the maps of Glen Tanar dated 1868 and 1901 showed that eight footbridges appeared across the Water of Tanar and the Water of Allachy between these dates. Were any of them Harpers bridges?

In the early nineteenth century, Glen Tanar was owned by the Marquis of Huntly, who also owned the adjoining Aboyne Castle Estate. He leased Glen Tanar from around 1870 to Mr Cunliffe Brookes, an industrialist and member of parliament from Lancashire. In 1888, Cunliffe Brooks bought the Aboyne Castle Estates, including Glen Tanar, from his daughter's father-in-law, the 11th Marquis of Huntly. Cunliffe Brookes developed Glentanar Estate as a sporting estate and was most likely responsible for awarding Harper & Co.'s fencing and suspension bridge contracts.

The Firmounth road was one of the old passes used by drovers between Deeside to the north and Tarfside on the North Esk to the south. It follows the left bank of the Water of Tanar for about 6 miles before crossing the river and scaling the bare granite shoulder of Mount Keen (3,052ft; 939m), the most easterly of the Scottish mountains over 3,000ft (914m), before descending to Glen Mark. In previous times the glen was home to several settlements and early maps show several stone arch bridges at Ess, Braelonie, Knockieside and over the tributary named the Allachy, linking with a bridge over the upper Tanar. There are five of these bridges in total, and all are present on the map of 1868. However, the first edition Ordnance Survey (OS) map of 1856 shows no footbridges in the area, although by the second edition of 1902 there are no less than eight.

I had discussed the possibility of these being Harpers suspension bridges with a colleague and local historian, Dr Pierre Fouin, who had been brought up on the Glentanar Estate and was engaged in writing a history of the glen. During his researches, Pierre asked an old school friend if he remembered any such bridges. The friend recalled crossing a very dilapidated bridge at Tanarmouth, where the Tanar joins the Dee, in about 1935. The two old friends repaired to the site and, sure enough, found the remains of a bridge on the right bank, a main cable still connected to a tensioner on which was cast 'Harpers Patent Aberdeen' (and see site 1 on the Outline of the Water of Tanar). The hunt was on. A photograph with a bridge in the background (and see site 4 on the Outline of the Water of Tanar) provided confirmation of another Harpers suspension bridge over the upper Tanar, most likely the one downstream of the bridge at the Halfway Hut (see site 5 on the Outline of the Water of Tanar). In addition, the footbridges at Glentanar House, the bridge a mile upstream at Black Ship and also the bridge at Shiel of Glentanar were visited. The remaining abutments all suggested a span that was likely to have required suspension, as were the two over the Allachy and its tributary the Gairney. Thus, of the eight bridges identified on the map of 1901, two were definitely the work of the Harper manufactory and the others almost certainly so, particularly in the context of the company's extensive fencing contracts throughout the estate.

The Tanar enters the Dee from the south, just a little west of Aboyne. We made our way through the wood to the confluence and eventually found a mast bearing a cable tensioner, held up at an angle by neighbouring trees and two fence posts on the east (right) bank, just as Dr Fouin had described (see Figure 34). We searched the area and found another rotted mast buried in the undergrowth, complete with its cable tensioner and an anchor cable attached by an eye bolt through the timber. From each cable tensioner the ¾in (19mm) galvanised steel catenary cables, with a ⅜in (9.5mm) hemp rope core, still fresh and in good condition, passed through the mast and down towards the river.

35. The remains of the bridge at Tanarmouth, showing the only example found so far of the small external tensioner. This was possibly the first Harper suspension bridge and was built some time between 1863 and 1871.

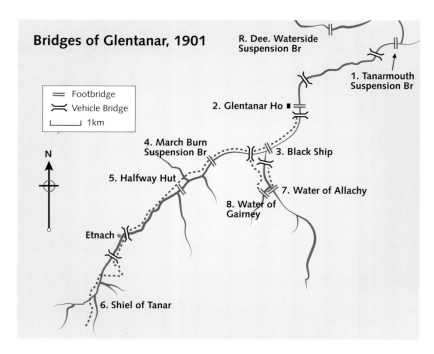

34. Outline of the Water of Tanar, showing the sites of bridges, from Shiel of Glentanar to the confluence of the Tanar with the Dee at Tanarmouth.

Bridges of Glentanar, 1901

R. Dee. Waterside Suspension Br

1. Tanarmouth Suspension Br

2. Glentanar Ho

Footbridge
Vehicle Bridge
1km

N

4. March Burn Suspension Br
3. Black Ship

5. Halfway Hut

7. Water of Allachy

8. Water of Gairney

Etnach

6. Shiel of Tanar

36. The site of the Harper foot suspension bridge visible in the background is unknown, but the bridge is thought to have crossed the Tanar near the March Burn (site 4 in Figure 34). The bridge shows large cable tensioners for the span cable and eye bolts for the anchor cables. The driver is probably Lady Glentanar, photographed in around 1927. *(Photo Glentanar Estate)*

Both cables could be traced downstream, one quite near the bank leading us to a third mast from the other side, now lying under the right bank. The cable measured 102ft (31.09m). The other catenary cable headed to the middle of the stream, where it may still have been attached to the fourth mast and its tensioners. Of the deck, its cables and tensioners, there was no sign. Returning to the site a few weeks later, we were surprised to find the nearer main cable in the river had parted and its attached mast was still lying free 100 yards downstream in an eddy. Its cable tensioner was retrieved before the next rain allowed the River Dee to carry it off for good. On further inspection, this cast was found to be labelled 'Harpers Pt No. 1 Aberdeen', a unique identifier.

This bridge at Tanarmouth bore similarities to that located further up the glen (see Figure 34) in that the cable tensioner for the catenary was balanced by an anchor cable fixed by eye bolts to the upper mast. Interestingly, both these Tanar cable tensioners involved approximately the same span, about 100ft (30.48m), yet were very different in size and capacity.

These differences imply that the Tanarmouth cable tensioners represented an earlier model, possibly also used for the shorter-span bridges placed upstream at about the same time. If the smaller was contemporaneous with the larger tensioner then, given the construction of the Ravenscraig bridge the following year, we can assume that Harper & Co. was making four designs of tensioner (including the fence strainers) during the years 1871 and 1872 at its foundry in Mealmarket Street.

More likely is that the Tanarmouth bridge was built before 1871 and the larger tensioner subsequently developed from it. How much earlier we cannot tell, but I believe that this bridge at Tanarmouth may be the earliest example of an externally applied cable tensioner, almost certainly dating from the late 1860s. However, there are some uncertainties surrounding this bridge. Firstly, the remains are downstream of the bridge's position on the 1920 OS map. Or did the OS get it wrong? Secondly, the remaining timber mast is in remarkably good condition to have survived for 150 years.

Close examination of the remains shows that the downstream anchor cable is still fixed to both its mast and its anchorage, and the upstream anchor cable has become detached from its mast, but is still attached to its anchorage. This suggests that the bridge may have been rebuilt on the present site, perhaps early in the twentieth century (Pierre Fouin's friend remembered crossing a dilapidated bridge as a young boy in the 1930s).

Two further suspension bridges were built about 1871 to this same pattern, over the Dee at Waterside near Aboyne, Aberdeenshire and further afield over the Cheshire Dee, at Shocklach. The former, an impressive suspension bridge, was located a mile above the confluence of the Tanar and the Dee.

RIVER DEE, NEAR WATERSIDE OF ABOYNE, ABERDEENSHIRE

The bridge near Waterside is unusual for its arrangement of two sets of main cables distributed between two sets of tension boxes, one of which was located at the top of the mast and the other halfway down. The span was an ambitious undertaking of 300ft (91.44m), representing by far the longest span to be suspended using cable tensioners (see Figure 37). Spans of this length became common twenty years later, by which time a construction technique utilising long cables that traversed from bank to bank suspended over saddles had become the rule. However, this was the first bridge for which the anchor cables were retained to the mast by their own tensioners on the mast, rather than by eye bolts. The site of this bridge is west of Aboyne, near Waterside (OS map reference NO493982, see Figure 34), over the Crofts Pool, and it would probably have been commissioned by the Marquis of Aboyne, the then landowner. Not only does the OS map show a suspension bridge, but the photograph in the archive matches the topography today. The angler reminds us that the Aberdeenshire Dee is a fine salmon river.

The suspension footbridge is seen on the OS map of 1902 and so we know that it survived into the twentieth century. We do not know how long it lasted, but major floods affected the Dee valley in May 1913, December 1914 and October 1920. The footbridge may not have survived these, especially if the original timber masts had not been replaced by steel. There is no sign of it in later OS editions. The deck cable profile is only slightly arched in this early bridge. The other Harper bridge of 1871 was constructed over another River Dee.

37. The bridge at Waterside of Aboyne, over the Crofts Pool. *(Aberdeen Art Gallery & Museums Collections)*

each mast, similar in appearance to those on the bridge at Waterside near Aboyne. Were these attachments for another set of perhaps smaller tensioners for second catenaries? This photograph shows no sign of a second set of cables. The bridge was commissioned by the Wynstay Hunt and also served the local community. The map of 1881 showed a 'footbridge' marked near Shocklach Green (this name being known from the company photograph) (SJ425505). We asked a local farmer, Robert Hale, about how best to approach the site. Robert occupied his grandparents' farm and had known of the bridge as a child. His next-door neighbour, who had recently moved to Ardnamurchan on Scotland's west coast, had a photograph of the bridge. We telephoned him, but he said that as he had moved, he had no idea where his copy of the photograph was. However, he knew of someone else who had a copy. Robert then kindly took us to another nearby neighbour, Jim Blake at Newhouse,

RIVER DEE, AT SHOCKLACH, CHESHIRE

The Cheshire Dee rises in Wales and, in its lower reaches, forms the boundary between Wales and England. Harper & Co. built two bridges over this river, one in 1871 (by John) and another about 1890 (by Louis). Records of the 1890 bridge 'over the Dee, near Chester' have so far eluded us. It was cited in Louis Harper's curriculum vitae for associate membership of the Institution of Civil Engineers in 1893.

The bridge of 1871 over the Cheshire Dee tells us that John Harper was no longer building bridges only locally. This bridge is likely to be that shown on the 1881 map crossing the Dee near Shocklach Green, and built for Sir William Matthias Williams Glynn of Rhuabon.

Shocklach is a small hamlet on the eastern bank of the river within sight of Wrexham. Its bridge, as illustrated, was built with timber pylons with cable tensioners. There are attachments of some kind halfway down

38. The Hunting Bridge at Shocklach, Cheshire, built in 1871. The fences at each side of the bridge presumably encouraged horses to commit to the crossing rather than to the River Dee. *(Aberdeen Art Gallery & Museums Collections)*

who knew more (he couldn't find his photograph either!). Although the 'Hunting Bridge' had collapsed before he was born, he recalled hearing that a worker had died during its construction and that 'they took his body up to a shed in a barn near here and left it overnight'.

Jim went on to explain that the east pylon footing could still be seen in a field, some way back from the present bank, and so, with the help of Robert and his son George, we found the spot. The concrete footing still held the stumps of the masts in its sockets, 4ft apart. The river meanders considerably in this stretch and constantly changes course. As a result, the

stumps of the west pylon became submerged. At a later date a fisherman's boat fouled it, sank and the man was drowned.

Since our visit, local resident Helen Arthan and her daughter kindly sent copies of the photographs of the bridge, taken between the two World Wars. They told us that a lack of agreement between the landowners at either end of the bridge had resulted in its gradual deterioration and eventual demolition. That it was demolished rather than collapsing into the river is evidenced by a local farmer's use of some of its ironwork as a tractor weight!

39. This is all that remains of the Shocklach bridge (1871) today. The river has changed its course, leaving the footing some way from the river. With the author's wife Janette are Robert and George Hale.

TORRY, RIVER DEE, ABERDEEN

This is the bridge that never was. However, it featured in an interesting chapter in Aberdeen's local politics. John Harper was returned to Aberdeen Town Council in 1868, aged 35, and became a leading light in the newly formed Party of Progress (Progressive Party). He had the distinction of being the first candidate ever to poll over 1,000 votes in an Aberdeen Town Council election. At that time the Town Council met in the former Town House that stood on the site of the present building, and was replaced in early 1871. This was a period of expansion in Aberdeen and John Harper was well known for his advocacy of the city's purchase of the lands of Torry, on the south bank of the River Dee, opposite the city. Indeed, this was the main plank of his election manifesto and a very controversial proposal, opposed by the then Lord Provost Alexander Nicol. When the motion to buy was put to the Town Council, the Lord Provost and his supporters lost the initial vote. This meant that the purchase was able to proceed, subject to the usual approval at a public meeting. The public meeting, or 'head court', was duly held and approval for the Council's decision sought. Despite a good deal of support from the floor, a disturbance occurred that allowed the Provost to dissolve the meeting before a vote was taken. As a result, the resolution to buy failed! However, after the Provost and his supporters had left the hall, seemingly victorious, Baillie Urquhart, the Senior Baillie, assumed the chair and continued the meeting. This time the resolution was passed unanimously! The squabble kept the Council occupied for some time, after which the consortium owning the Torry Farm estate, including Milne of Kinaldie, Sir Alexander Anderson and the Menzies Trust[32] pulled out because of the unreasonable delay. They sued the Council for failing to complete the sale, but were told tersely by the Provost that the adoption of the resolution at the head court had, in any case, been illegal and so there was nothing over which to sue! However, good sense prevailed and, later in 1869, the lands were purchased to allow expansion of the city.

John Harper demonstrated his commitment to the cause. In 1871, during his last year on the Council, he offered to place a bridge across the Dee in the line of what is now South Market Street, at his own expense. This offer was declined in favour of the construction of a substantial road bridge – the Victoria Bridge – which was not completed until a decade later. In the intervening years people who wished to cross the river at this point relied on the transport of the cable ferry boat, which ran a regular service from Torry to the north bank of the river until, on 5 April 1876, allegedly overloaded and facing a brisk wind against tide, the ferry became inundated on its way across the Dee and capsized with the loss of thirty-two lives. John Harper was also to build the first industrial unit on the purchased Torry lands, at Craiginches. In 1871, as a result of the Municipality Act of that year, ward boundary changes compelled the whole Council to retire. Despite being pressed to stand again, John decided to pursue other interests.

OVER THE GREAT NORTH RAILWAY AT HOLME, HUNTINGDONSHIRE

This bridge, possibly the Harpers' earliest railway footbridge, was built in the 1870s, at Holme, on the Great Northern Railway (GNR) line just south of Peterborough (TL196876) although its precise date is not known. This account comes from the *Peterborough Advertiser*:

FOOT SUSPENSION BRIDGES

On Monday last, a new suspension bridge (known as Harper's Patent Foot Passenger Bridge), placed across the Great Northern level crossing at the Railway Station, was opened to the public. The bridge, which is of recent invention, is said to possess the combined principles of suspension, tension and arch, and was originally designed at the request of several owners of extensive coffee plantations in Ceylon, Africa, and elsewhere, for the purpose of spanning rivers, ravines etc. It has also been adopted by several noblemen and gentlemen in Scotland, one erected on the Marquis of Huntly's estate at Aboyne, crossed the river Dee with a span of 300 feet. The one just opened has a span of 80 feet, with 6 feet clear width for traffic, and is light and pretty in appearance; a decided improvement upon the unsightly wooden structures erected for the same purpose over some of our railways. As a proof of its portability and simplicity of construction, we may state that it was erected in seven days, without in any way interfering with the traffic on the line, which at that point is very considerable, upwards of 1300 trains (including shuntings) passing under whilst in the course of construction. The work was executed under the personal supervision of Mr John Harper, of Seafield House, Aberdeen, the patentee.

40. This railway footbridge at Holme, Huntingdonshire, over the GNR, may represent the earliest such bridge built by the Harpers. *(Aberdeen Art Gallery & Museums Collections)*

The bridge is basic in design, using timber for the masts and tensioners for the usual deck, main and anchor cables. It is similar to the bridge at Lincoln, built later.

These press cuttings are mines of information. One can almost imagine publicist John Harper dictating his text to the lineside reporter. In this article is the first mention of the possible origins of this application of the patent – the coffee plantations of empire in Ceylon, Africa and, intriguingly for our researches, 'elsewhere'.

By 1879, the works at 12–14 Mealmarket Street were becoming inadequate so Harper & Co. relocated to the Albion Works with its enhanced facilities. In the company's promotional material of the time, suspension bridges are mentioned for the first time, although Harper & Co. had been manufacturing them for a decade. Possibly the first bridge to emerge from the Albion Street works was that to be set over the River Don at Monymusk, Aberdeenshire.

RIVER DON, AT MONYMUSK, ABERDEENSHIRE

The Seventh Baronet of Monymusk, Sir Archibald Grant, was one of several local estate owners who asked Harper & Co. to bridge the River Don in Aberdeenshire, in an area known locally as Paradise. The bridge

is seen here looking north from the left bank, upstream towards the hill of Bennachie (NJ679179). The main cables pass through timber masts to reach the corresponding tensioner boxes mounted on the bank side of the masts.

The *Aberdeen Daily Free Press* of Tuesday, 28 October 1879 described the scene:

NEW BRIDGE OVER THE DON AT MONYMUSK

We have just received from Messrs Harper & Co., of the Albion Ironworks, Aberdeen, an admirable photograph of the really handsome wire bridge the erection of which they have just completed at Monymusk. The pitch of perfection to which the patentees have now brought their wire bridges is specially noticeable in this, the last of these structures which has come from their hands. The span is of no less than 107 feet, while the breadth is 4 feet. These bridges, light, airy and elegant as they appear in construction, are really of great strength. They are constructed on precisely the same principle as the common suspension bridge, and their safety and utility have been proved not

41. This bridge at Monymusk, Aberdeenshire, was built in 1879 to cross the River Don near Paradise. *(Aberdeen Art Gallery & Museums Collections)*

only in all parts of the country, but also in India and the colonies, and, indeed, at the present moment the patentees are engaged in the construction of two bridges of similar design for Australia. In this particular instance the bridge, which has been erected by Sir Archibald Grant of Monymusk, will be of great use to the ordinary wayfarer and also to the tenantry on the estate. The bridge is distant about two miles and a half from Monymusk station, and is close to the entrance of the grand old forest, so widely known by the name of Old Paradise. The special purpose of its erection is to facilitate intercourse between the two sawmills of Ramstone and Ord Mill, which are on opposite banks of the river, and the connection between which had up to this time been effected by a rude bridge of trees supported by a large boulder in the centre of the stream. The scenery all round about is particularly fine, and the bridge seems to add to rather than detract from the beauty of the scene. The erection of the structure was superintended by Mr John Harper, of Seafield, and as showing the skill and celerity with which such work may now be carried out it may be mentioned that the bridge was fitted up and ready for use within a fortnight.

The bridge initially had timber masts, probably constructed of larch from the estate, but at some stage they were replaced by I-shaped steel beams and Harper finials were added. The design of the finials indicates that this is likely to have taken place in the late 1890s.

The bridge continued in operation until around 1970 when the Ord Mill finally closed. It then gradually fell into disrepair, as may be seen from the later photographs. Each Hogmanay, normally sober and upright members of the community could be seen making their annual crossing on the remains of the cables. The bridge was removed in 2005.

The Monymusk bridge enhanced the beauty of the countryside, as did others. Thomas L.F. Burnett of Kemnay (1885–1940) refers to the 'shakkin' briggie' in verse four of the poem 'Paradise' as he describes the approach to the Paradise woods:

42. The 'swing bridge' at Monymusk, showing that the timber masts have been replaced by paired 'I' girders complete with the Harper finial atop. The tensioning arrangements are clearly seen, but the bridge is now derelict (2005).

As you go doon the Lord's Throat
On Paradise ye come,
The bonny Don a' round it
Reflects the setting sun.

The purple heather carpets
The slopes of Bennachie;
The firs stand out like sentinels
For all who came to see.

The beauties of the country
God made for tired man
Who each his road must travel
Since ere the warl' began.

The peat reek rises frae the burn
Of cottar house an' mill;
The shakkin' briggie stands alone
And a' the earth is still.

(Thomas L.F. Burnett of Kemnay, 1885–1940)

Alexander Inkston McConnachie, a local author, wrote several travelogues of the north-east of Scotland in the 1890s. In his book on Bennachie, published in 1890,[33] McConnachie describes the approach to Bennachie from the station at Monymusk as leading over this bridge towards the southern slopes of the hill.

The late Jimmy McIntosh of Ordmill lived his whole life beside the Monymusk bridge. He told me of it being crossed by horses and riders and of a bull being brought across to the cows. On the return journey, the bull was less than enthusiastic and recourse was made to the ford a few hundred yards downstream at Blackhillock. Betty Lawie of Blairdaff recalled two local lads who habitually crossed the bridge on motorbikes on their way to work, just as large numbers of Nepalese commuters do today on the bridges in Nepal. The principal purpose of the bridge was to provide estate workers with the means to cross the Don between the bobbin and grain mills of Ord and Ramstone. The stone bridge at

Boat Cottage, half a mile downstream, was not built until 1906, when it replaced a ferry. Five miles downstream is our next bridge.

RIVER DON, AT BURNHERVIE, ABERDEENSHIRE

We do not know exactly when the bridge at Burnhervie near Kemnay, was constructed, although it shares similarities with the Monymusk bridge. In 1979 the bridge is described by the Aberdeenshire county engineer as having suspension cables above, tension cables below (for the deck) and stay cables (to the anchorages). The suspension cables and tension cables were secured and adjusted by capstan-type winches at the top and bottom of the stanchions (masts), respectively, at both ends. The stay cables used the same type of adjuster at the column top and were cast into the anchor block at the bottom. This description matches exactly the design of the Monymusk bridge nearby. Burnhervie's timber masts had been replaced by steel beams, probably about the same time as those at Monymusk.

43. This bridge over the River Don at Burnhervie features curious recesses in the abutments facing the river on both sides, which are still present today.
(Aberdeen Art Gallery & Museums Collections)

The Burnhervie bridge collapsed in 1979 during a charity raft race when the upstream anchorage cable on the left bank failed. Local farmer Henry Smith was present that day, standing upstream on the left bank. He reckoned that about eighty people had crowded onto the bridge and were moving from side to side as rafts passed below. Suddenly, the bridge sagged, but failed to quite reach the surface of the water, allowing the crowd to retreat dry to either bank. The mechanism of failure is reminiscent of that at Lees' second bridge at Galashiels, but this time without any report of a broken 'cutty'!

The original owner of the bridge is not known, and its purpose is not clear. However, local man Duncan Downie recalls that, at the time, Kemnay was a 'dry' town and workers from the nearby granite quarry had nowhere to slake their thirst apart from at the licensed shop across the river at Burnhervie.[34] Initially they made their way there by stepping stones, but no doubt this was hazardous, particularly on the return journey from the drinking shop. The hazard may or may not have been ameliorated by fellow workers holding the hands of anyone they considered to be slightly unsteady and, as one story has it, of pinning an inebriate to the ground with a block of granite to prevent him from crossing the river alone. The bridge joins the lands of the Burnetts of Kemnay and the Fetternear Estate and they may have shared the cost. Harper & Co. fenced parts of the latter estate about that time and, as we have seen in Glen Tanar, fencing and bridges seem to go together. On the other hand, the bridge may have been commissioned by the owner of the licensed premises who had most to gain. Kemnay gained its own pub in 1937.

After its collapse in 1979, the original Burnhervie bridge was replaced in 1980. Its successor had the same general appearance, but used tubular iron columns rather than the previous 'I'-beam sections. This bridge was regularly vandalised and was itself replaced in 2005 by a rigid-deck, cable-stayed bridge, the design of which echoes that of its predecessors.

44. The first bridge to be constructed at Cromdale, Morayshire, over the River Spey, was built in 1881. A possible tardiness with maintenance led to its demise in a high water in 1892. (*Aberdeen Art Gallery & Museums Collections*)

CROMDALE, RIVER SPEY

Cromdale is found on the River Spey just downstream of Grantown-on-Spey. The parish church of Cromdale and Advie stands on the east bank of the river. The Cromdale bridge was built adjacent to the church (NH066290) in about 1881.

John Harper Jnr refers in correspondence to photographs taken of this bridge. He had several photographs taken from the Grantown side but he really wanted to achieve a view from the Cromdale side. Not happy! One of the photographs that caused John so much discontent, taken from the Grantown side looking towards the church (right), is shown here.

The photograph shows that the bridge was located just above the ferry mooring at Boat of Cromdale (the boat mooring is in the foreground), an area of the bank clearly recognisable today. The bridge reached the right bank just at the lower end of the churchyard. It was built by local subscription to a fund, of which the Reverend John Grant, of Cromdale Manse, was treasurer. By 13 August 1881, local farmers had carted and earthed the boulders required for the footings of the bridge, fortunately at their own expense. A week later, the *Grantown Supplement* of 20 August 1881 reported that:

… under the personal superintendence of Mr Harper and Mr John Harper, Engineers, Aberdeen … and the work, it is expected, will be finished within a month. There is to be a grand amateur concert in behalf of the funds for the Bridge in Cromdale Public School on Tuesday evening, the 24th inst. We have seen a list of those who are kindly to perform and seldom is such musical talent gathered together. No doubt, there will be a crowded house.

On 10 September 1881, the *Supplement* recorded:

Passengers are now crossing the new foot Bridge, and it is expected to be entirely finished in two or three days. The workmanship is very elegant and substantial, reflecting great credit on the Engineers – John Harper & Son, Aberdeen – one of whom has personally superintended the work from the commencement.

And, a week later, the *Supplement* again:

CROMDALE BRIDGE

The suspension passenger bridge over the ferry was finished on Thursday afternoon. The Committee are, we are glad to understand, entirely satisfied with the work. They took a great interest in it in the course of erection, and besides the great trouble they have had, they are handsome subscribers. Now that the bridge is completed, the careless observer has no idea of the work that has been done. There are thirty-six tons of stone out of sight, to which the wires on either side are securely fastened. The Messrs Harper, Aberdeen, were the Engineers, and they are to be congratulated on their highly successful work. John Harper, Esq, of Seafield personally superintended the operations from the beginning and saw that everything was done in a substantial way. The appearance of the bridge is most graceful, and besides its usefulness, it is an ornament in one of the loveliest parts of our Strath. The right Honourable the Earl of Seafield and the Directors of the Great North of Scotland Railway company have visited it and been much pleased. It has a clear span of one hundred and ninety-five feet. The walking platform measures over two hundred and forty-six feet. The whole consists of galvanized steel rope wire. It has an arch of about 4 feet and stands considerably above the flood mark of 1829. The erection took just a month. The debt on it we learn is about £50. No doubt it will soon be lessened by the subscriptions of friends and otherwise. The Treasurer is Rev. John Grant, Cromdale Manse.

The flood mark described by the *Supplement* refers to the Muckle Spate of 1829, which marked the highest water recorded to date in the rivers Dee, Don and Spey in north-east Scotland. In Huntly, 4in (95mm) of rain fell in twenty-four hours. The upper Dee was spared, suggesting the downpour could have been in the Muick and Lui Glens with the waters sweeping into the valley of the Dee, raising its level by 27ft (8.2m). During the same night of 3–4 August, the waters of the Spey were similarly affected; this remains the highest flood height of these rivers to this day.

The Cromdale bridge was built to a basic design and used larch masts and three large external cable tensioners per mast. However, by 1892 successive spates by this great river had led to scouring round the footings and some of the suspension rods required attention; remedial work was put in hand.[35] Although the bridge had been built at a height above the river that took account of the 1829 spate, problems arose on the night of Friday, 30 January 1892:

As stated last week, some concern for the safety of the Bridge was entertained: but it was erroneous also to say that the repairs upon it had been completed. The workmen on Friday had only concluded the first stage of the repairs by temporarily bracing the loose suspension rods. The principal part of the work was to follow, and the contractors left their tools on the river side, intending to resume the following morning. What the workman found when they next visited the scene of their labours the next morning was – a flooded river, approaching in height the flood of 1829, and only a vestige or two of the structure upon which they had been employed on the previous day. The catastrophe was complete: their tools had also been swept away by the flood. The wreckage of the bridge is for the most part in the bottom of the Parson's Pool, and evidently connected by the wire rope to the pillar lying prone on the left bank of the river. Who will have to undertake the labour of clearing it away?

(*Grantown Supplement*, 6 February 1892)

This last question is answered by an invoice for the 'use of steam engine drawing Cromdale Footbridge from the bed of the river Spey to bank' dated 21 February 1892! The Dowager Countess of Seafield paid the requisite £3 3s 0d.[36]

Another impressive span negotiated by Harper cables and tensioners resulted in an aerial ropeway erected as a preliminary to the building of the railway bridge at Garmouth, near the estuary of the Spey, for the access of men and materials. This description comes from the *Moray and Nairn Express*, 29 December 1883. It is included here as testament to the power of the bridge cable tensioner:

THE WIRE SUSPENSION RAILWAY ACROSS THE SPEY

This novel scheme of transit over a rapid part of the Spey, 500 feet wide, near the new railway works at Garmouth, was successfully completed on Friday. We mentioned a few weeks ago that an additional steel rope was to be added in order to ensure perfect safety. This has now been fitted up, and a new design of light iron carriage has been adopted instead of the original wooden one. The new carriage, which is neatly and strongly constructed, weighs only 140lbs. It is 4 feet 8 inches long by 2 feet 6 inches wide, and 1 foot 7 inches deep. It is lined and floored with strong diamond lattice wire, thereby presenting little or no resisting surface to the wind. On the top, at each of the four corners of the carriage, is a V grooved pulley, 15 inches in diameter. The carriage has thus the appearance of an ordinary carriage inverted. The wheels on each side run on the two upper ropes, and they are kept in position and locked in the V groove by the weight of the carriage, which, with its load, is suspended below the centre of gravity during the passage. The four upper wheels have each a crank handle affixed, by means of which the passengers, seated back to back, can propel the carriage up the short incline at the termination of each journey. For 400 feet or thereby the trip is accomplished by gravitation. The third rope introduced is placed at a lower level, under the centre of gravity. It passes through a single pulley inside the carriage, close to its floor. This under cable is strained up to sustain one half of the prescribed load, and is equal in strength to both the upper ropes, the combined breaking strain of the whole being equal to 32 tons, according to the Admiralty test. Immediately on the third rope being strained up to its proper level, and the new carriage put in position, Mr Harper of Seafield, who had been entrusted by the Great North of Scotland Railway with the design and execution of the scheme, started for the opposite shore, which he reached in the short space of forty seconds, returning with a passenger, against a strong pressure of wind, in rather less than a minute, without having to use any exertion except in ascending the few feet on incline as he approached his destination. The ropes are suspended from Scotch fir posts, the tops of which are 15 feet above the level of the river. They are 12 inches in diameter, fixed in the ground, and stayed by rope of equal strength to that of those crossing the river. They are securely anchored in pits, with 25–30 tons of ballast. The whole work of the span was executed by Messrs Harper & Co., Albion Iron Works, in a few days and fitted up in less than a week – including the time of travelling from Aberdeen – by three mechanics, superintended by Mr Harper of Seafield, whose patent bridge winding apparatus contributed essentially to the completion of the undertaking with so little loss of time. The invention, which, we believe, costs a trifle compared with the cheapest style of footbridge, should commend itself to all who wish to get the nearest and quickest way over wide rivers, ravines etc. and we understand that Mr Harper, who has proved adept at such works, is holding himself in readiness to erect a span of 1,000 feet to carry the same load.

This underlines the importance of the Harper patent wire strainer in generating the tension required for long spans. There is no record of the construction of further aerial cableways, although they are by nature usually temporary.

RIVER ERICHT, AT CRAIGHALL, BLAIRGOWRIE AND RATTRAY, PERTHSHIRE

This bridge was built in 'about' 1886, according to Louis Harper. The bridge is just below Craighall Castle over the River Ericht (NO174483). My wife and I visited the area in August 2006 when Mr and Mrs Rattray, descendants of the purchaser, kindly directed us to the site. Here, the River Ericht descends through a steep gorge incised into the old red sandstone conglomerate, the cliffs of which can be clearly seen on the photograph. Access to the bridge required us to follow a fishermen's path along the east bank upstream from a lower reach. Fortunately, the river was low or it might not have been possible.

We first came upon several cable tensioners of familiar appearance, lying in the shallows of the river. Looking about, we saw that the wreckage of almost the entire bridge festooned the cliff of the left bank from their attachment above. We found a path leading to the footing above and there, in the undergrowth, we came across one of the pylons, complete with cables and tensioners still attached. This finding allowed us to study the way in which the cables passed through the timber pylons (and each

45. This bridge was built just below Craighall Castle over the River Ericht in 1886. The bridge was released from its western (left) anchorages when it became unsafe in the 1950s and now lies against the cliff on the right. *(Aberdeen Art Gallery & Museums Collections)*

other) to access the rear of the tension box. There being two boxes at this level on opposite sides of the pylon, the cables crossed and probably made contact in the innards of the pylon. The bridge had a span of 90ft (17m).

The bridge gradually fell into disrepair, having been in use for about sixty years. The cables can still be seen on the west bank and they look as if they had been cut, leaving the bridge to fall and lie below the east bank attachments. This would have been about 1950. Local gillie Damian O'Neil recalls crossing the remains as a boy with his friends long after it was safe to do so, 'Boys will be boys,' he said.

46. These remains show the top of one of the Craighall masts and demonstrate the back-to-back arrangements of the cable tensioners. The cable to each approached from the other side, passing through the timber to gain the spindle onto which it was wound. This would tend to support the attachment of these heavy objects to the masts.

OVER THE GREAT NORTHERN RAILWAY AT OFFORD, CAMBRIDGESHIRE (*c.* 1887)

Sixty miles north of London, the GNR passed through Offord. Although we have confirmed that the photograph is indeed of Offord Station, we have no further information about the fate of the bridge (TL217671).

The line in the picture was quadrupled in 1887 and the increased span required by four tracks no doubt accounted for the tower arrangement, similar to that seen on the bridge built at Queen's Park, Chester, in 1832.

The picture shows the completed bridge, but its poor definition fails to show the cables and so the deck and the persons crossing it appear to be defying gravity. It is uncertain whether the towers were built of steel or wood, but it more likely they were of the latter. Cable tensioners are seen mounted at the tops on both sides of the towers to take the main cable and the anchor cables. The tensioners for the deck cables are mounted beside the stairs as they reach the tower. There are no finials. These features are reminiscent of bridges constructed before 1887, but this bridge was

clearly built to span the new layout of four railway lines at Offord, a work that was still in progress as an 1887 photograph of the GNR line nearby at Sandy, south of Offord shows only a double track at that point.[37] This bridge must have been built in early 1887 just before Louis Harper joined the firm because there is no mention of it in his curriculum vitae.

RIVER NAIRN, AT NAIRN, MORAY

The first bridge in which Louis Harper was involved was built at Nairn in 1887 (NH886562), the year of Queen Victoria's Jubilee. Louis stayed with a Mrs Shepherd of Amhurst Villa in Cawdor Street, a house that still stands. Two weeks were required to prepare and build the bridge. However, it seems that Louis may have been running a little late because his father came up the weekend before the opening to complete the latticework of the side rails, 'a tedious stage,' he said. Although the erection was overseen by Louis, the bridge was built to a John Harper design. Its opening was a festive affair:

> Provost Leslie and Colonel Fraser first crossed the Bridge, and on their return, Colonel Fraser said: 'In the absence of Sir Alex Dunbar, whose absence we all regret very much, all I can do is to declare this beautiful Suspension Bridge open. The bridge as you all know is erected in momento of the Jubilee of our Sovereign the Queen. Nairn has many amenities – it is beautifully situated; it has the finest climate in the world; and it is inhabited by the very best of people (hear hear). It is therefore no wonder that Nairn offers so many attractions to the visitors. While we have many beautiful walks at the seashore; and along the banks of this rippling river, the bridge cannot fail, I am sure, to add to the amenities of the town. I hope Sir Alex Dunbar and members of his family will on many occasions cross this bridge. The family of Boath has always been in sympathy with the people of Nairn, and I trust this bridge will form another band of union between the town of Nairn and the estate of Boath. I need not detain you further under the hot sun, and will now declare the Bridge open.' (cheers)
>
> (*Nairnshire Telegraph*, 22 June 1887)

47. This bridge crosses the GNR at Offord, Cambridgeshire. (*Aberdeen Art Gallery & Museums Collections*)

The figure above shows a striking view of the bridge by the Victorian photographer George Washington Wilson.

THE NAIRN, FROM THE RAILWAY BRIDGE, 11,759.   G.W.W.

48. Jubilee Bridge over the River Nairn, at Nairn. (*University of Aberdeen, George Washington Wilson Collection*)

The press report continues:

The bridge is of a singularly graceful and pleasant aspect. The span is exactly 100 feet, the wire ropes are suspended from heavy pillars on each bank of the river. At a little distance it looks like a spider-thread crossing the stream. In truth, however, it is a very strong and durable bridge, although constructed of light materials, of some hundreds of tons of resistance strength. The vertical rods between the platform ropes and the suspending cables add immensely to the strength as well as to the beauty of its appearance. Ornamental wire netting lines the sides of the bridge, which is substantially floored with close-jointed timber. The rapidity with which the structure was put together was very remarkable; a fortnight of actual work was all that was required, the secret being that all the parts of the bridge were actually made ready to their actual lengths and sizes before being taken to the ground. Powerful winding barrels tighten the whole structure, so that there is very little of the oscillation or shakiness to be found in most suspension bridges. These barrels are a patent of Messrs Harper, Aberdeen, the builders of the bridge. The spot where the bridge has been erected is immediately opposite the Farina Mills, the wreck of which it is very desirable should be removed, since it is very unsightly. The one end of the bridge rests on the Boath property and other on the town's land. It is a symbol of the good relations that subsist between the House of Boath and the town of Nairn. The scene all around is lovely and the people of Nairn are only realising the fact that they have in the river-side a most charming spot, of which any town in the Kingdom might be proud. Standing at the approach to the Suspension Bridge, and looking down the stream, we have here looking through the noble arches of the railway bridge, some pretty views of the town.

The bridge at Nairn lasted until September 1915, when there was very high water in many of the rivers of north-east Scotland. On 28 September 1915, the *Nairnshire Telegraph* reported:

JUBILEE BRIDGE CARRIED AWAY

The suspension bridge across the river below the cemetery, erected as a memorial of Queen Victoria's Jubilee, was carried away overnight. It was standing on Saturday evening, but on Sunday morning all that remained of it were the supporting posts on the right bank of the river. The pillars on the town side had apparently given way, and the ironwork was swung across

49. The Harper brothers. **(a)** John Harper (1833–1906). (*Aberdeen Art Gallery & Museums Collections*) **(b)** Hugh Harper (1831–1912). (*In Memoriam, Aberdeen*)

the river where it lies in a mass in the pool. The bridge was a great public convenience, and its destruction is a cause of much regret.

Louis Harper's glorious suspension bridge was replaced by a tubular steel bridge built shortly afterwards, which, in its turn, was washed away in 1956, to be replaced by a precast concrete monstrosity. However, let us return to earlier times.

NEW BEGINNINGS

In 1885, a couple of years before the erection of the Jubilee Bridge amid great rejoicing at Nairn, the partnership between Hugh and John Harper had been dissolved. Correspondence at this time from John Jnr is mildly disparaging about Hugh and his colleagues in the wire-working side of the business (John refers to his uncle and co. as 'Haddenites', a reference to their activities at their separate site in Hadden Street) and suggests some strain within the family. Hugh left Thorn Villa at Seafield for a house in nearby Great Western Road at about the same time, reinforcing his need for a little more space from his younger brother. They had left home together over forty years earlier, and had lived and worked closely ever since. For the Harper brothers, 1885 represented the parting of their ways.

Hugh continued to trade as Harper & Co. 'Iron gate and wire fence makers, blacksmiths, wholesale retail wireworkers and hardware merchants'.[38] Around 1872, Harper & Co. had moved to Hadden Street, near the Green at the heart of the old mediaeval town, and maintained works at Mealmarket Street and Forbes Street. In his later years Hugh was joined as partner by William S. Pirie, who took over the business on Hugh Harper's death in 1912. Hugh was an original trustee of Mannofield parish church. He and his wife Margaret Meldrum (1834–1925) had eight sons and three daughters, of whom three sons, George, James and Peter, survived childhood, along with two daughters, Alice and Jessie. His younger son, Peter, graduated from Aberdeen University in medicine in 1895. Harper & Co. ceased to feature in the Aberdeen Street Directory after 1931.

In 1885, John Jnr set up, with his father, Harpers Limited, with works continuing at Albion Street. Harpers Ltd functioned as general founders, specialising in power transmission systems for mills both locally and abroad. The company also continued to build suspension bridges designed by Louis Harper.

Although John Harper had ostensibly retired in 1876, it is clear that he had merely stepped aside a little to let John Jnr run the business. He remained the major shareholder and was always on hand to offer advice. For example, it was John Snr who erected and demonstrated the aerial railway at Garmouth in 1883, supervised the erection of the Monymusk (1879), Birkhall (1880) and Cromdale (1881) bridges, and helped with the completion of the Nairn bridge in 1887. It is doubtful that any strategic decision was taken without John Snr's approval. However, responsibility for the day-to-day management of the foundry now rested with John Jnr and thus his father was free to pursue other interests. In his later years, the young lad with radical tendencies who had led industrial action in the

1850s became a staunch conservative. In an instalment of its series entitled 'Our portrait', the *Northern Figaro* wrote of John Snr in 1886:

> His abilities are esteemed and his person liked by all with whom he comes in contact, and if the man who makes two blades of grass grow where only one grew before deserves the thanks of humanity, Mr Harper, who has introduced and perfected a new industry in the locality and thus afforded employment to many hundreds of people, cannot fail to have the community deeply grateful to him.[4]

Louis joined Harpers Ltd in 1887, following his apprenticeship, just in time to cut his teeth on the erection of the Nairn bridge. For the next eighteen months he served as bridge manager within the firm and during this time built bridges at Crathorne in Yorkshire, Darwin Harbour in the Falkland Islands and over the River Dee near Chester. Like the bridge over the River Nairn, all of these were built to John Harper Snr's design, and for this reason they are included in this chapter. Of these three, we have information on only the first, at Crathorne.

50. Crathorne Hall. *(James Crathorne)*

RIVER LEVEN, AT CRATHORNE, TEESIDE

We approached Crathorne Hall from the north, towards its rear, after a drive through extensive grounds. The long south front of the hall, complete with classical pediment, is very impressive.

This bridge was commissioned by Lionel Dugdale (1862–1941). It crossed the River Leven, which runs through the Craven Estate. Lionel went on to build Crathorne Hall in 1903, which was the largest English country house of the Edwardian era. His father, John, had bought the Estate in 1844 and Lionel inherited it on his death in 1881. Lionel's son, Thomas (1897–1977), became the first Lord Crathorne in 1959.

Beyond the south lawn there is a steep slope to the river, which today is crossed at this point by a fisherman's bridge. This current bridge represented one of a series of replacements for the Harper bridge, which had been built a little upstream. We found the slope covered by an impenetrable mixture of bramble and hawthorn, which discouraged further exploration – an early return to the bar was preferred! Crathorne Hall is now run as a country house hotel and retains many of its period features intact. The management still includes members of the Crathorne family, who vacated the premises in 1977.

The suspension bridge, which measured 4ft (1.22m) in width and 55ft (16.76m) in span, was designed by Louis Harper and built by Harpers Ltd at the Albion Works. It was basic in design. It had six pairs of cable tensioners in all, most likely mounted on timber masts. This elegant bridge was washed away in the great flood of July 1930. Since then, at least a couple of replacement bridges have been put in place, but have suffered similar fates as a result of the instability of the river banks.

Only eighteen months after joining Harpers Ltd, Louis left to set up an independent civil engineering practice, initially under the title of the

51. The suspension bridge built over the River Leven, Crathorne. (*Aberdeen Art Gallery & Museums Collections*)

Harper Bridge Co. It may be that, having been trained as a civil engineer and architect, Louis felt somewhat limited in designing suspension bridges only and wished to engage in a wider practice involving the development of public works and private housing.

Louis' departure from Harpers Ltd marks the end of bridge building according to John Harper's style. It was now Louis' turn to develop his own style, albeit he used and extended the engineering principles developed by his predecessors, whereby the stiffness of the structure is enhanced by the use of cables of the opposite curvature.

6

A Certain Style: The Bridges of Louis Harper

It is light, graceful in outline, and withal strong.

(George Menzies, Trentham)

When Louis Harper was born in 1868, his half-brother John Jnr (1855) was by then aged 13 and his half-sister Lizzie (1852) was 16. Louis' early education took place at the Gymnasium in Old Aberdeen but he went south to Nelson College, Lee in Kent for a year in 1880. In 1881 he returned to Aberdeen and entered the Aberdeen Grammar School in its splendid new building in Skene Street, where he remained until 1883. Louis was then apprenticed to Jenkins & Marr, Aberdeen, architects and civil engineers, from 1883 to 1887. In 1887 he joined Harpers Ltd as bridge manager for the firm, but remained only eighteen months. In 1889 he set up his own practice at 115 Union Street as a civil engineer and architect, briefly under the title of Harper Bridge Co. Presumably he saw attachment to a foundry managed by his elder brother as rather limiting for someone qualified in both architecture and civil engineering. The Harper bridge business was transferred to Louis, and thereafter his maker's plates referred to 'Louis Harper, Maker, Aberdeen, Scotland', although the bridges continued to be manufactured at Harpers Ltd ironworks. Louis continued to have a close association with Harpers Ltd, designing the company's new foundry, and particularly with its development of the motor car in the 1890s.

Some idea of the extent of Louis' work at this time may be gleaned from the Candidate Circular submitted prior to his election as an Associate Member of the Institution of Civil Engineers, to which he was elected in 1893:

> He has served a Pupilage of 3 years and 8 months in the office of Messrs Jenkins and Marr, Civil Engineers, Aberdeen (1883–87), during which time he has had experience in the surveying, levelling and preparation of Drawings connected with the extensive surveying of water- and sewerage-works, bridges, and other minor works. He was subsequently employed by Messrs Harpers Limited, Engineers, Aberdeen for 1½ years as Manager of the Bridge Department of their business, designing and erecting Bridges over the Rivers Nairn, at Nairn; Dee, near Chester; Darwin Harbour, in the Falkland Islands; and Tees, at Crathorne, Yorks. Since 1889 he has been practising on his own account, and during that time has built Bridges over the Great Northern Railway at Lincoln; Rivers – Bandon, at Bandon, Cork; Feugh, at Banchory; and Carron, at Falkirk. He has also designed and erected the new Engineering Works of Harpers, Limited, which cover an area of nearly 4 acres. In 1892 he assisted the Town Council of Aberdeen in the surveying, levelling and preparation of Parliamentary plans and sections connected with new water scheme.

From 1889, practising independently, Louis stamped his own style on the bridges, this evolving steadily over the next decade. The transition from

52. Louis and Alice Harper, c. 1895.

53. Pedestrian footbridge over the GNR at Lincoln. The masts look to be of wood with finials at their tops. The deck cables have cable tensioners at the masts at deck level and the main cables pass over saddles to reach the ground anchorages. (*Aberdeen Art Gallery & Museums Collections*)

the bridges of John to those of Louis is evident at Lincoln, Bandon in County Cork and Banchory in Kincardineshire (now Aberdeenshire); we will first look at these.

The most notable change was the abandonment of the Harper Patent cable tensioner for the main and anchor cables and its substitution by a continuous cable that ran from anchorage to anchorage, over saddles at the masthead. These cables would have been adjusted by staple screws at the anchorages, which represented another departure from the traditional Harper style. However, cable tensioners were still used for tensioning the deck cables and the system of suspension was unchanged. Louis' adoption of this standard configuration of main cables used by all other manufacturers presumably reflected his formal training as a civil engineer.

OVER THE GREAT NORTHERN RAILWAY AT LINCOLN, 1890

The bridge at Lincoln, the third Harper footbridge in the GNR system, built in 1890, is illustrated as showing timber beam masts linked by transoms of similar material. These are finished by a smooth domed

saddle, atop of which is the Harper finial, making its first appearance in what appears to be its final form. The deck, of 70ft (21.34m) in span, is arched, supported by cables tensioned at the mast foot by the Harpers' patent cable tensioner. Wooden steps and balustrades complete the access.

Matching the photographs with town plans for 1913, this bridge was most likely sited at the Pelham Street Junction, at Lincoln Station (SK977707). It is no longer there and there is no record of its fate.

RIVER BANDON, AT BANDON, IRELAND, 1890

All Louis Harper's business stationery made mention of a bridge in Ireland. We found that it was at Bandon, in what is now the Republic of Ireland. Bandon is a small town 20 miles south-west of Cork. It is included here rather than with bridges erected overseas in Chapter 7 because, at the time it was constructed, all of Ireland was part of the UK.

The River Bandon powered several mills in and around the town, all of which initially served the textile industry. One of these mills, bought by George Allman in 1804, lasted only a short while until it was converted to a distillery in 1825 under the ownership of the Allman family. The bridge was commissioned by Mr J.C. Allman and erected on site in 1890 by George Armstrong, a local civil engineer.

George A. Armstrong, civil engineer, Bandon, Cork, reported in 1890:

> I return herewith the two pliers, as I have completed the lattice work. The Bridge, 120 feet span has been well tested by storm and flood with very satisfactory results. I take this opportunity of saying that all the material sent out from your Works was put out of hands in a most satisfactory manner, and the gates you supplied well and neatly finished. I am well pleased with this Bridge and Mr Allman, for whom I act, has asked me to say the same from himself.

The bridge is very similar to that at Lincoln, built the same year. Here, however, the masts are constructed of steel 'I' beams which terminate in the saddle carrying the main cable, which runs continuously between the anchorages. The masts are completed by an early example of the sphere and cone finial that was to become Louis Harper's architectural signature. There are subsidiary anchor cables attached to the masts. The deck is of

54. The bridge built over the River Bandon for George Allman (who is probably the figure on the bridge). The masts appear to be steel (for the first time) and show full-length main cables over saddles and cable tensioners for the deck cable. (*Aberdeen Art Gallery & Museums Collections*)

wood supported on cables that are axially tensioned at the foot of the masts. The deck curve is pronounced so that its shape almost mirrors the form of the main cable.

Mr Eddie Goggin, editor of the *Bandon Opinion*, kindly arranged for us to visit J.C. Allman's house, Ardnacarrig, in 2007. Ardnacarrig House stands high on sloping ground above the right bank of the River Bandon; its park runs right down to the river. In earlier times J.C. Allman had constructed six grand flights of stone steps that passed down through sloping lawns to his suspension bridge. This is the route he used each morning as he went to work at his distillery on the opposite bank of the river. For many years now, the lawns have been unmaintained and the steps have become but a memory. Mrs McArthur, the present owner,

55. Alnacarrig, Bandon, with steps leading down to the bridge. Altman's brewery on this side of the river. *(The Bandon Opinion)*

indicated where we might find some steps in the undergrowth, and under the canopy of a low tree, we found one of the flights. It gave us a glimpse of a lost world and was enough to provide a line on the bridge site, where a photograph taken about thirty years ago had highlighted a solitary anchorage. However, search as we might, we could not locate any sign of the remains of the suspension bridge.

The distillery was not the first industrial venture for the Allman family, which had made a brief foray into cotton production at the close of the seventeenth century. However, the family found themselves unable to compete with the Lancashire textile industry and thus their mill at Oldtown, on the western edge of the town, was gradually wound down, finally closing in 1825, by which time the distillery was up and running. The distillery today stands abandoned and partly demolished. One of the buildings remains in use, but most are gaunt and empty, prey to spreading ivy and the elements.

In his application for membership of the Institution of Civil Engineers, Louis Harper refers to a bridge having been built 'near Chester', again,

probably around 1890. No trace has been found of this bridge to date. Had it had wooden masts it may not have lasted more than fifty years. It most probably stood on the estate of the Duke of Westminster at Eaton Hall, although today, unfortunately, the estate has no record of the bridge.

RIVER FEUGH, NEAR BANCHORY, ABERDEENSHIRE, 1893

The third bridge in this transitional phase was built in 1893 for Mr John Douglass of Tilquillie, Feugh Cottage, Banchory, Aberdeenshire, who wrote, 'I wish to express to you my entire satisfaction with the Bridge you put up for me over the Feugh. It fully comes up to my expectations.'[39]

This bridge stands just upstream of the Falls of Feugh and the present roadbridge over the river. Today, it remains in private use and is listed by Historic Scotland. It is clearly visible from the road. Ann Taylor, the present owner, kindly allowed us to visit the bridge in 2006 and again in 2014. The main cables pass across saddles from anchorage to anchorage and the deck is tensioned by cable tensioners fixed to the masts, as can be seen at the foot of the mast. The bridge has a span of 100ft (30.48m) and a width of 4ft (1.22m). Its original timber masts have been replaced by 'I' beam girders and it has recently been redecked.

When it was first erected, the deck had a notable arch, and the pillars were rough timber with the roots of the branches still showing as a decorative effect. Yet while the old Harper tensioner was in evidence for the platform cables, the timber posts were topped by the new arrangement of a saddle and finial, unlike any other timber post we've come across. Next, of uncertain date is the George Washington photograph (see Figure 26), where the pillars appear to be different – either of timber again or even cast tubular iron. The arch is still there, but is less fully intact. Again, the posts have changed, this time to 'I' section steel and the deck is horizontal. What has been the effect of the loss of arch? The bridge today (see Figure 56a, right) is perfectly firm to cross but presumably would have been even stiffer if the arch had been retained.

56. (a) This private bridge over the River Feugh, Banchory, Aberdeenshire, initially had wooden masts which were later replaced by steel
(b) (*Overleaf*) There are cable tensioners at deck level and the main cables pass from bank to bank.

57. Contrast the arch of the deck of the Feugh bridge when first built with its appearance today in Figure 56. See also Figure 26. (*Aberdeen Art Gallery & Museums Collections*)

HARPERS' CRAIGINCHES IRONWORKS

Having established his own practice as a civil engineer and architect in 1889, Louis became involved in surveying for the new water supply and sewerage works to be developed in Aberdeen, as well as for the laying out of streets. One of his earliest commissions was in 1892 to design and build the Craiginches Ironworks for Harpers Ltd. Louis continued to run his enterprise on his own until 1896, when he was joined by George Sutherland, a local architect. This partnership was to be responsible for the construction of houses in Aberdeen's expanding West End, as well as several country schools and a large block at 55–60, Bridge Street, Aberdeen. However, by 1901 the partnership had been dissolved. Thereafter, George Sutherland formed a partnership with James M. Pirie, which traded until 1914. After his father's death in 1906, Louis moved his professional address to Seafield, as his letterhead of the time shows.

By 1890 it was apparent that the Albion Works of Harpers Ltd was becoming inadequate. Having explored the possibility of extending the works to include a property on the other side of Albion Street, John Harper sought a new site on which to develop a state-of-the-art foundry. Louis designed and built the new foundry at Craiginches, on

58. Louis Harper's company motto 'River, Railway & Ravine', adopted as the title of this record, is seen here on his letterhead.

59. Motor-driven wheel lathe at Harpers' Craiginches Ironworks. *(Aberdeenshire Council)*

60. A detail from the town plan of 1900, showing Harpers Ltd Ironworks at Craiginches, Aberdeen, and its connections with the Caledonian Railway.

the southern approach to the city; it opened in 1892. It would employ some 400 men, making it one of the largest employers in the city at the time. Not all were pleased at having to leave the city centre site for a greenfield location 2 miles away. Some years later, in 1907, the Institution of Mechanical Engineers visited Aberdeen and attended, amongst other firms, the Craiginches Ironworks of Harpers Ltd. This is an account of that visit:[40]

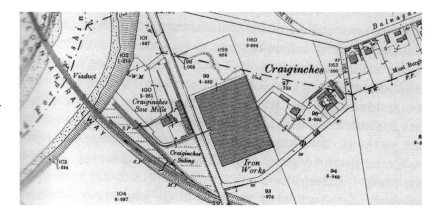

These works, situated on the south side of the River Dee, and about 1¼ miles from the joint passenger station of the three railways entering the city, were erected in 1892 to meet the increasing demand for the various productions

61. The interior of Harpers Ltd Ironworks at Craiginches. (*The Engineer*)

62. In 1900, Harpers Ltd was the main agent in Scotland for Benz. (*Charles Nichol*)

specialised, the leading manufactures being rope and belt pulleys and fly-wheels, toothed gearing, high class steel shafting, bearings and their supporting fixings, and generally all accessories required for the transmission of power. The premises are lighted electrically by 55 arc lamps, aggregating 75,000 candle power, and are served by 28 travelling cranes on 2 miles of overhead rails, whilst the machinery is driven by 28 electric motors; The premises have a roof area of 3 acres.

The Foundry proper is arranged into two bays, 35 feet and 25 feet wide respectively and three bays, each 18 feet wide, all 260 feet long, the two larger being furnished with three electric travelling cranes, two of 20 tons and one of 8 tons carrying power. In this department are two cupolas with melt 9 tons and 6 tons per hour respectively, and conveniently arranged for rapid manipulation are numerous gear-wheel moulding machines and special rope-pulley grooving machines, capable of an output of 100 tons of castings per week.

The Turnery, which has an area similar to the Foundry, is connected with the latter by bogie rails for the rapid transport of castings to tooling operations, and is equipped with special shafting lathes, milling machines, keyway slotters, shaft key-grooving machines, modern boring and turning mills etc all driven off four lines of shafting, each divided and operated by two electric motors stationed in the bay divisions, thus giving clear space for the many overhead travellers.

Harpers Ironworks was the first factory to be constructed in the greenfield site that has since become East Tullos Industrial Estate and the first factory in Aberdeen to have electric light. The site was bounded by Wellington Road to the west, Girdleness Road to the south and Balnagask Road to the north. In addition, the foundry was served by a siding off the Caledonian Railway, which allowed the import of pig iron and the export of castings (see Figure 60).

In 2006 Charles Nichol, formerly of the Harper Motor Company and grandson of Charlie Harper (second son of John Jnr and the chairman of Harpers from 1918 until 1960), encountered a customer named Tony Weller, purely by chance. Once Charles' connection with Harpers had been established, Tony revealed that he had served his apprenticeship at the Craiginches ironworks and would be happy to share his experiences with us.

Viewing the photographs of the foundry taken in 1907 took Tony Weller back to his days at Harpers in the 1950s. In the fifty years from its construction, the foundry did not change much at all – its earthen floor, the timber posts that supported the roof and the shaft and belt-driven machinery had all remained in place. Again, looking at the range of products shown in the advertisement of 1908, Tony recognised most of them as being in production in the 1950s. About 90 per cent of the foundry's output was destined for use in paper mills, mainly locally. When the Craiginches Ironworks were developed, Harpers had the largest lathe in Aberdeen at the time: it measured 33ft (10.06m) between centres and allowed the forging of wheels up to 20ft (6.10m) in diameter. Wheels of smaller diameter were cast in one piece, but those of larger diameters were cast in two halves that were subsequently bolted together. This also facilitated their insertion anywhere along an existing power transmission system. The sand of the cast was skimmed with 'plumbago' or graphite, an alloy of lead and iron, to ease the cast from the moulding box.

Most of the wheels were then machined. The inner surfaces were machined first and the wheel was then mounted on a mandril to allow for the milling of its outer edges. When fine tolerances were not required, the teeth were cast rather than being milled.

Tony Weller described the use of the key seater. This basic tool was used to cut a slot in the inner aspect of the wheel's central aperture and also on the shaft to which it was to be attached. Each pair of slots combined to form a square section, although the combined slot might taper to allow the key to be driven tight. The concept of locking moving parts together with a key was basic to Harpers' power drive transmission systems, as it had been to both the wire strainer and, later, the bridge cable tensioner. John Ross, chairman of the Harper Motor Co. from 1969–96, relates the story of John Jnr having come out of retirement at almost 60 years of age to look after the works during the 1914–18 Great War. He used to stand by the door of the works at the start of the day and would reportedly say to any late-comer, 'You look tired, man. Away hame an' sleep it aff so that you can rise and maybe be in time the morn!' Bang went a day's pay! During the Second World War the works manufactured munitions, as it may have done during the First World War.

By the mid-1890s, Harpers' had developed its bridge building activities into a very successful line of manufacture. However, it is interesting that the company appeared to make no move towards developing bridges capable of taking a carriageway wider than 8ft (2.44m). Perhaps these lightweight, easily portable bridges suited the light engineering nature of a business located in a part of the country that necessitated the import of iron and steel from a distance, and manufactured bridges to be exported.

It is ironic that the same foundry was fabricating early motor cars that would render the footbridge largely obsolete. John Jnr and Louis embraced the 'horseless carriage' with enthusiasm. A partnership between John, John Jnr and Louis to develop the motor manufacturing business was established around the mid-1890s. This partnership later became the Harper Motor Company.

We now come to a group of very similar bridges, which marked a major departure from the earlier Harper design. All had tubular cast iron masts, possibly in tribute to the enhanced casting and milling facilities at Craiginches. It will be recalled that Louis had switched to using conventional main cables over saddles. Now he shared the main anchorages with the deck cables, discontinuing the use of the Harpers' patent cable tensioner, on which the fortunes of the firm had originally depended. At the anchorage, the main and deck cables each had their own adjusting staple screw. Finally, all of these bridges sported Louis' masthead finial. Bridges following this pattern were built at Falkirk, Grimsby, Trentham, Sellack near Ross-on-Wye and at Cromdale on the Spey, between the years 1893 and 1895.

RIVER CARRON, AT FALKIRK, STIRLINGSHIRE

The River Carron passes the northern edge of Falkirk on its way to join the River Forth near Grangemouth. Just a mile below the Harper steel wire foot suspension bridge was the Carron Ironworks, the famous foundry at the heart of the industrial revolution in Scotland. The ironworks was a major exporter of pig iron at this time and it is possible that the iron masts of the Carron bridge had their metallurgical origins nearby.

The bridge, built amidst surrounding parkland (NS866813), had a recreational rather than a strategic purpose, and this continued to be true until recently. Here is the contemporary report published in the *Aberdeen Evening Express* of 27 June 1893:

FOOTBRIDGE OVER THE RIVER CARRON

We observe from the *Falkirk Mail* that a Harper's patent steel rope suspension bridge has been erected near Falkirk. The bridge is 90 feet span by 4 feet wide, and was opened on Wednesday by the county Council of Stirlingshire

63. The bridge over the River Carron at Falkirk. (*Aberdeen Art Gallery & Museums Collections*)

64. An early form of the common anchorage, at Falkirk.

in the presence of 2,000 to 3,000 people, who passed over it. The bridge was supplied by Mr Louis Harper, CE, Aberdeen, whose design was selected by the committee out of several others submitted. A service of cake and wine took place at the opening ceremony; and in the evening the inhabitants of the village held a demonstration in honour of the occasion. Remarks were made by various speakers, who referred in high terms to the beauty and stability of the structure.

Presumably all of the '2,000 to 3,000' people would then have subsequently crossed and re-crossed the bridge and so it would have been well tested. These events were clearly red letter days.

This bridge clearly shows the early form of the common anchorage for both deck and main cables. In Figure 65, the main cable is attached to the staple screw by a disc and stirrup arrangement, and the deck cable has the more conventional swaging of the cable onto a carrier that is, in turn, threaded onto the adjustable staple screw.

The transom proudly bears a plate inscribed 'Louis Harper CE, Maker, Aberdeen'. Louis was, at this time, 25 years of age. This bridge survived until recently despite annual floods by the River Carron (Figure 63). Unfortunately, it had lost its finials, which added a certain style to its appearance. This bridge, known locally as the Dorrator Bridge, was replaced (2014) by a modern beam bridge. As a monument to the much-loved 'swing bridge', the pylons on the right bank have been retained with the finials replaced. An information board has been placed nearby. This is the only Harper bridge known to have a pipe tune composed in its celebration – 'The Dorrator Bridge'!

65. The Falkirk bridge before its removal in 2014. The finials have been removed. Note that the horizontal deck would have allowed more motion than it was designed for.

RIVER TRENT, AT TRENTHAM, STAFFORDSHIRE

This bridge looks identical to that over the River Carron at Falkirk and was built in the same year (SJ868397). As the photograph shows, its deck features a graceful upward curve, a conspicuous feature of Harper bridges. The undergrowth in the photograph prevents us from establishing whether the deck was tensioned to the base of the pylon with a tensioner or passed beyond to a common anchorage, but the latter is more probable.

George Menzies, Commissioner to His Grace the Duke of Sutherland, Trentham Hall, Trentham, Staffordshire, wrote, 'The Suspension Bridge of 70 feet span, which you recently erected for the Duke of Sutherland, in the gardens at Trentham is a thoroughly satisfactory structure. It is light, graceful in outline, and withal strong. It serves its purpose well and conveniently.'[39]

This bridge was removed in the 1930s when the gardens were developed for public use. An art deco stone bridge was built a little way downstream and around this time Trentham Hall was demolished.

RIVER FRESHNEY, AT GRIMSBY

Three bridges were built over the River Freshney at Grimsby when the Duke of York Public Gardens were laid out in 1894 (TA262096). Two had spans of 50ft (15.24m) and one of 35ft (10.67m); all were 4ft (1.22m) in width.

Marshall Petrie, AMICE, Borough Engineer and Surveyor to the Corporation of Grimsby, Town Hall, Grimsby, Lincolnshire, wrote:

66. The bridge at Trentham Gardens. (*Aberdeen Art Gallery & Museums Collections*)

67. One of the three bridges built over the River Freshney within the Duke of York Public Gardens. Although the deck cables cannot be seen, it is likely that they shared an anchorage with the main cables. (*North East Lincolnshire Council*)

In reply to your letter of the 8th inst., with reference to the three Steel Rope Suspension Bridges recently supplied by you to this Corporation, and erected over a stream in the Duke of York Public Gardens, I am pleased to say they have so far given great satisfaction, and have been much admired for their neat appearance.[39]

These bridges became well known to local people, among whom some younger members preferred to cross the decking outwith the suspenders, their posteriors suspended above the water. The bridges were replaced in 1978 by concrete and beam constructions, much to the dismay of the more romantic citizens. I received a message from Bruce Lincoln of Grimsby to say that the smaller 35ft bridge that crossed the river to an island in its midst appeared to be still in place, although boarded up. This information gave me and my wife an excuse to visit Grimsby and the Duke of York Public Garden. We found the bridge to the island had been replaced like the others, but that the original masts at the landward end had been retained as a feature and that the maker's name on the transom was clearly visible. At the base of the masts were cableways for the deck cable, confirming that both catenary and deck cables had used a common anchorage.

RIVER SPEY, AT CROMDALE, HIGHLAND

This bridge replaced the Harper-built bridge of 1881, which had been washed away (see Chapter 5). The original bridge had its footing on the bank, but its replacement was built on piers, one of which was based on the east bank and the other either bordered the west bank or even arose from within the river at that side. We do not know definitely that this replacement was a Harper bridge, but it seems likely. The masts are of tubular cast iron and there is a cable below the nearer approach, which may be a deck cable on its way to the main anchorage on the bank. A similar deck cable can be seen in another view of this bridge, representing strong evidence that Harpers built the new bridge. Controversially, it was built a couple of hundred yards upstream of the previous bridge (NJ066289).

It appears that the previous bridge had been something of a nuisance to the minister. He had supplemented his living by having fishermen as

68. The second bridge to be built over the River Spey at Cromdale was somewhat controversially sited a little upstream of its predecessor. (*Moray Museum*)

69. The bridge between Sellack Boat and King's Caple, just upstream of Ross-on-Wye. The original cables at the anchorages and saddles have been strengthened. *(Barbara Nash)*

guests who wished to have access to Parson's Pool, over which the bridge spanned. The disturbance of pedestrians crossing the bridge affected the fishing and thus, presumably, the fishermen were not sorry to see it go. The *Grantown Supplement* of May of the following year informs us that the local committee had undertaken to replace the bridge, but:

> …are in a fair way to messing the matter a second time.
>
> They have fixed upon a fresh site for the bridge, for the bad and very insufficient reason that the minister of the church adjoining wanted it so. The minister is on the committee, and pressed his point without scruple.
>
> It is creditable to those of the Committee who resigned rather than seem to acquiesce in an arrangement which sacrificed the public interest to the private aims of the individual, and that individual not of a particularly elevated type. Although one may not be disposed at the last glance to credit it, the position of the last bridge interfered to some extent with the letting of the Manse, and with the minister's revenue from that source.
>
> His reverence lets, along with the Manse, the right to fish in the pool which was spanned by the bridge; and pedestrians, it would appear, in crossing to and fro, disturbed the fish in the pool beneath, as well as the fishers in the Manse who fished the pool.
>
> This is the explanation of the change of site. We are much afraid that the Committee will receive little pecuniary support from the Cromdale public when are considered the selfish action of the minister, the peculiar methods of the builders already at work upon the structure and the questionably secure foundations upon which the main supports of the bridge are laid.

Clearly there was little love lost between the editor of the *Grantown Supplement* and the Reverend John Grant! Predictably, the *Grantown Supplement* did not record the opening of the replacement bridge in 1894 and therefore we are denied critical information about that event, including definitive information on the builder of the bridge.

It is a little puzzling that there isn't anything in the wider press about the re-establishment of this crossing. Possibly a replacement wasn't as big an occasion to warrant a press report.

Today only the footings survive, the bridge having been replaced in 1921 by a girder road bridge built by Dorman Long of Middlesburgh. The road bridge crosses the River Spey on a bearing of 295 degrees, whereas the OS map of 1908 (revised edition) indicates that the suspension bridge crossed the river on a bearing of 270 degrees and thus today, one footing is to be found downstream and the other upstream of the present bridge. The east footing, buried in undergrowth, is in line with the old road that passed along the boundary wall of the churchyard.

RIVER WYE, AT SELLACK, HEREFORDSHIRE

The trail defined by our family's bridge-building heritage has led us to some of the most beautiful parts of the UK, and none more so than the valley of the River Wye. We visited Sellack in September 2005. The day was fine and we had a beautiful view of the bridge as we came over the hill and down to the church at Sellack, some 2 miles north of Ross-on-Wye (SO564280). There were two fields of sheep to cross between the church and the bridge, with a grass track and stiles between the two. The bridge has a span of 190ft (57.91m) and the deck is 6ft (1.83m) wide. The deck is supported by cables with axial tension to the common anchorages. The pylons are of tubular cast iron, linked with Louis Harper's maker's transom. A plaque on the abutment bears the date 1895.

We returned to the church and my wife, who, as a daughter of the manse, is always curious about the interiors of church buildings, went in and found an exhibition about the bridge. Included was an account of the early history of the bridge:

> Not all was peace and jollity however – with King's Caple a daughter church to Sellack, it was not always easy for the vicar, who lived in Sellack, to reach the other village. Originally a ford and then later a ferry, the crossing could be difficult.
>
> The boathouse, the residence of the ferryman, (the family name was Harris) is still on the King's Caple side. Certain boatmen could be very awkward (and often were), refusing to take the vicar across! (One cleric is reported to have frequently crossed the river on stilts.) This continued strife caused much local outcry and resulted in a public petition for a bridge to be built. This was finally done due in main to the energies of the Rev Augustin Ley (1877–1908) and largely at his expense! A fine suspension bridge. Under the bridge is a stone built into the buttress with the inscription – 'To the honour of God and the lasting union of these parishes'.

70. Finials to Louis Harper's design, consisting of a sphere with horizontal and vertical bands with a cone atop, all made in one casting, and the maker's plate are clearly seen, although reinforcements have been added across the saddles, which are now somewhat crowded. *(Barbara Nash)*

Once again it is the local church that mobilises support for the building of a bridge. The bridge was commissioned from Harpers and its erection supervised by architect Mr Ernest G. Davies, MSA, Hereford and opened in 1895. Hereford County Council took the bridge over six months after it was opened.

In the church we also found a local parish magazine telling of a recent 'Annual Bridge Service'. This turned out to be a service of thanksgiving for the crossing, which presumably has taken place regularly since the bridge was opened. It has obviously been appreciated by the clergy and others.

The bridge continues to be well maintained by Herefordshire Council, which kindly supplied me with copies of the original plans. In them can be seen the longitudinal decking layer that is missing from today's bridge, although the camber of the deck is clearly seen. Attached to the cables are some extra strengthening cables, clamped to the original. At some time these appear to have been applied to points of wear, such as on the saddles, anchorages and the points at which the deck cables pass through the cast iron masts. When these were applied is not known. This is the finest example of a Louis Harper bridge that remains in use in the UK and is listed under Ancient Monuments.

The next four bridges to be built show architectural rather than technical development. The masts become a tracery of lattice steel, whereas the cables retain their previous configuration and comprise full main cables that share the main anchorages with deck cables. In 1892–93, two bridges were built over the Aberdeenshire Dee with lattice masts – Polhollick (Abernethy) and Abergeldie (Blaikie Bros). The adoption of lattice masts represents the final phase of Harper bridge design and was to become the norm for bridges to be built later in India, Nepal, South Africa and Estonia. The size and weight of the earlier tubular masts were quite unsuited for export to underdeveloped regions of the world and this may have dictated the switch to lattice steel. Unlike the earlier tubular masts, lattice steel masts could be transported already fabricated or, more usually, in parts.

who had taken on the responsibility of cost would be glad to be relieved of a liability which should not be theirs. He asked that all adults do what they could to discourage injury to the bridge. Mr Lowther handed a key to Mrs Marshall and also presented her with a photograph of the bridge as a souvenir – Mrs Marshall then declared the bridge open, and after the cheering had subsided Mr Marshall returned thanks for the compliment which had been paid to Mrs Marshall. The party having crossed the bridge to the road behind the Keswick Hotel, Mr Wood begged to publically acknowledge their indebtedness for the liberal support that had been given to the committee, as well as to Mr Lowther for his earnest and persistent work in the fulfilment of a pledge, and to Mr Hodgson for his advice and assistance in the placing of the bridge. Mr Lowther briefly responded. He had been reminded of a big contract; but one bridge was there and another would come in due time. The Rev J.N. Hoore thanked

RIVER GRETA, AT KESWICK, CUMBRIA

We visited Keswick in September 2005, but our enquiries did not, at first, get us anywhere. However, we later followed up a lead and made contact with Mr Jeff Taylor, who gave generously of his time and effort in researching the bridge. The bridge was commissioned by the Cockermouth, Keswick and Penrith Railway in order that the people in the new houses being built between Penrith Road and Ambleside Road on the left bank of the river could more easily access their railway station on the right bank.

In 1898, the *Lakes Guardian & Keswick Visitor* reported:

The 'Lowther' Suspension Bridge

This new bridge was formally opened on Monday night (18.07.1898) by Mrs R.D. Marshall – Mr Highton said they might congratulate themselves in having acquired a bridge which in no way detracted from the scenery but rather opened out one of the prettiest river views on the bonny Gretna. It would be useful to workmen, the visitors, and the people generally. For the site they were indebted to the generosity of Mr Marshall (who had also given a handsome subscription) and the Fitz Trustees. The bridge had been made by Mr Harper of Aberdeen, and the design and arrangement spoke volumes in its favour. The cost had been considerable and there was still about £60 to raise and those

71. The bridge over the River Greta at Keswick, the first Harper bridge to be constructed with lattice masts. *(Aberdeen Art Gallery & Museums Collections)*

72. The stump of a mast is still visible at Keswick. The Harpers plate is half covered in concrete. *(Jeff Taylor)*

Mrs Marshall for the gracious way in which she had performed the opening ceremony and cheers followed.

The bridges of Louis Harper at this time were even more arched than those of his father and this view of the Lowther bridge shows this well. The bridge, which was 90ft (27.43m) in span and 4ft (1.22m) in width, was eventually decreed unsafe and closed in 1979. It was removed thereafter. The approaches and footings are still in place, including the stump of one of the pillars on which the Harpers Ltd plate can be seen half covered by concrete.

RIVER DOVE, AT DOVERIDGE

Not far away from Trentham in Staffordshire, the village of Doveridge lies on the east bank of the River Dove (which separates the counties of Derbyshire and Staffordshire), opposite Uttoxeter, occupying rising ground above the flood plain. The photograph we obtained showed a suspension bridge over a river of a certain size, with a church spire a little distance away on rising ground, amidst trees. Most of the churches in the area had towers and thus the church spire at Doveridge was a possible match. After examining the area around the Dove bridge, we walked downstream along the left bank towards Doveridge and the most likely site.

As we approached, in the distance, we saw a suspension bridge but our doubts about it being a Harper bridge grew as we came closer. This was not the bridge in our photograph, but it did stand on the same site. As we discovered, the present bridge was built by David Rowell & Co. of London, in 1945.

We made contact with Tom Deville of the local heritage society. He told us that the original bridge had been commissioned in 1898 by a Mr F.A. Brace of Doveridge Hall as the price he was required to pay in order to divert a public footpath around rather than through his land. Subsequently, the whole estate had fallen into disrepair and the hall itself had been demolished in 1938. The bridge had been neglected and been replaced in the mid-1940s by a similar structure by David Rowell & Co. Images of the earlier bridge confirmed it as having been built by

73. The Harper bridge at Doveridge, built in 1898. (*Aberdeen Art Gallery & Museums Collections*)

that crossed a bridge in the photograph served the mine (and didn't cross the river) and a ridge on the hillside above represented the line of an earlier railway. However, the driver had no knowledge of the suspension bridge in the foreground of the picture. He suggested that we go down to the farm at the old mine and then walk down a track which would pass under the railway bridge and into the middle of the site of the bridge shown in the photograph.

We parked the car at the gate of the farm and made our way across the yard and through the gate at the far side. As we walked down, we found ourselves on the remains of a tarmac road. However, our first disappointment was that the ironwork of the railway bridge didn't match that shown in the photograph. Passing under the railway bridge, our second disappointment was that there was no sign of footings on the bank beyond. Were we in the right place?

Louis Harper and although it was thought that some of the components of the original bridge had been retained in the present structure, close comparison of the masts shows that they are of different construction. Then it was off to Wales and our next bridge.

RIVER TAFF, AT ABERCYNON, WALES

Abercynon is a post-industrial town in the Taff valley, which features numerous reminders of its more prosperous past as a coal mining community. We identified seven footbridge crossings in the area and checked them all, but none of them was a suspension bridge. Coming across a roads department vehicle, we asked one of its drivers if he recognised anything in the photograph we had acquired of the bridge on its completion. After some head scratching, he said he thought he recognised the hillside as that above the old Navigation Mine. The railway

74. The bridge constructed near the Navigation Mine, Abercynon, in 1900 had a width of 6ft (1.83m) and a span probably in excess of 200ft (60.96m). We approached this site from the far side, coming under the railway bridge to the river. (*Aberdeen Art Gallery & Museums Collections*)

We returned to meet a very irate farmer who did not want us on his land. (I had forgotten that we were in a foreign land! In Scotland, responsible access through farmland is accepted.) I tried to placate him by saying that we'd heard that there had once been a suspension bridge down that track. 'What of it?' he demanded. We retrieved the photographs from the car and, once again, let them work their magic. Soon the farmer was telling us that although the bridge had been before his time, he had been told that miners had used it to go to the pit and that courting couples would include it in their evening walks. He pointed out other changes to the scene in the photograph that had occurred in the intervening 110 years, particularly the vegetation that had grown up around the now disused railway. 'And the bridge ironwork?' I asked, 'Oh, they replaced the deck in the '50s,' was his reply.

The bridge, built around 1900, had become victim to floods in 1942 (ST080938). The farmer had known of it from a book in the local library and he directed us there. The book is unfortunately out of print but the copy in the library showed us three pictures of the bridge, including that illustrated in Figure 74.

NEWQUAY ISLAND BRIDGE, CORNWALL

A frequently photographed Harper suspension bridge is that at Newquay Island on the Cornish coast – it is not difficult to see why. It connects a sea stack to the shore, providing a footway 75ft (22.86m) above the beach at low tide. Newquay Island is prominent from the town and a good view of the bridge can be seen as the ravine opens up. I was surprised to see that the pylons had been encased in concrete, above which the finials peeped out. Otherwise the bridge appeared to be in good shape. Access to the bridge was by a private gate painted blue, but there was no means of raising the occupants of the house on the island.

Initially, when we visited, the small blue gate inset into the white wall above the steps was as far as we could get. So near… We established that the house was owned by Viscount and Viscountess Long, whose telephone number was ex-directory. We took photographs from various angles and, while down on the beach, noticed a young couple crossing to the island. We placed a note of introduction, with our telephone number, in the letterbox.

75. The bridge at Newquay Island today. This bridge was built to allow access to the sea stack and may have crossed the 'ravine' of Louis Harper's logo 'River, Railway & Ravine'. *(Ewen Cowan)*

By the next morning we hadn't heard anything, but Janette insisted that we should simply go down to the grass outside the gate and wait. Sure enough, the young man returned across the bridge but stopped two thirds of the way across to gaze out to sea. This went on so long that his intention to cross the bridge and emerge from the blue gate came into some doubt. However, in time he did so and Janette approached him and told him of our mission. He said that he was a guest in the house and was bound for his car with some luggage as he and his fiancée were leaving. When he returned to the house, he would let the owners know we were waiting to see them. In due course the viscount came across the bridge and welcomed us to Newquay Island. As introductions were made, the young couple passed us and their hosts explained that they had become engaged on the suspension bridge the previous evening. His lingering on the bridge obviously represented a romantic reminiscence!

The Longs couldn't have been more welcoming and were very interested in what we could tell them about the bridge. Our family understood, but could not confirm, that it had been commissioned by Sir Hal Caine, a Victorian novelist, as a means of crossing to a summer house on the island. Another possibility was that it was built by the Island Estates Authority, who owned the island at the time.

It was 100ft (30.48m) in span and 4ft (1.22m) in width and would therefore have cost £150, according to a price list issued two years prior to its construction in 1900. The bridge pylons were constructed of lattice steel and would have been fabricated at the Craiginches Ironworks and loaded onto a train in the company's siding off the Caledonian Railway. The maker's plate was obscured by the subsequent concreting of the pylons to protect the structure from the salt spray. The anchorages were of the common type, holding both the main and deck cables. Lord

76. The common anchor for the main cable (left) and the deck cable (right) on the bridge at Newquay Island. (*Photograph: Helen Long*)

Long said that on stormy days the bridge bounced all over the place 'like a kangaroo', but a recent insurance inspection had given it a clean bill of health. So even with the Harper 'suspension, tension and arch' configuration, stiffness is only relative. However, it may be that the tensioning required some adjustment!

Lady Long wrote later to say that the maintenance of the bridge was undertaken by a rope access firm, and a neighbour got a shock one morning to see a 'body' hanging below the bridge on the end of a rope. On another occasion the Newquay Rowing Club Singers lined up along the bridge to sing songs including 'Home from the Sea'. I hope the tide was out and the sea calm for it must have been a magical evening.

A local press report described the arrival of the bridge in 1900:

> Mr Louis Harper A.M. Inst. C.E., of Aberdeen, can fairly claim that his steel rope suspension bridges may be seen all over the world, in places as far apart as India, Cape Colony, the West Indies and Ireland – not to mention many parts of our own little island – the graceful but strong structures for which Mr Harper's name is well known, may be seen spanning some mountain torrent, or peaceful stream, or serving as a footway across a railway line. One of the latest specimens of Mr Harper's skill may be found on the west coast of Cornwall, where he has connected Newquay Island with the mainland by a bridge of 100 feet span. The fact that this is exposed to the full force of the westerly gales bears testimony to the excellence of the work.

This bridge of 1900 at Newquay Island is illustrated in this fine photograph from the George Washington Wilson Collection of the University of Aberdeen. Wilson (1823–1893) was an Aberdonian photographer of some renown, who ranged far and wide throughout the UK and had contracts with Queen Victoria and Prince Albert. By the time of his death he employed forty and was one of the largest photographic publishers in the world. His company survived him until 1908. You will find his photographs of the Nairn and Feugh bridges also in this volume. Newquay is the last of the bridges in the UK so far identified as having been built by Harpers Ltd. Of the four lattice-masted bridges in the UK (Keswick, Doveridge, Abercynon and Newquay), this is the only one to survive and, frustratingly, the lattice work cannot be seen. On the other hand, two of the five surviving UK Harper bridges had tubular cast iron posts (at Birkhall and Sellack), which represents a tribute to the lasting power of that material. However, Louis Harper's lattice design was also incorporated in two suspension bridges built by James Abernethy & Co., which do survive.

James Abernethy & Co. was an Aberdeen engineering and foundry firm (the oldest foundry in Aberdeen, dating from the late eighteenth century) which latterly occupied premises on Wellington Street at the north end of the Wellington chain bridge (Sir Samuel Brown, 1831), with works at the Ferryhill Foundry nearby. The connection between Louis Harper, civil engineer, and Abernethy's suspension bridges is circumstantial. It was known that Louis Harper and the manager Mr J. Morrison Wyness (father of the local architect and historian Fenton Wyness referred to in Chapter 1) worked on projects together and, according to Margaret Harper (Louis' daughter-in-law) this professional connection continued into the 1930s. James Abernethy & Co. was well established as a maker of truss bridges, particularly for railways, but also for roads. Abernethy built a notable suspension bridge at Dumfries in 1875 with twinned catenary cables of linked bar chain, associated with the name of John Willet as designer. The use of single steel wire cables on the bridges over the Dee and Spey mark a departure from this design. Louis Harper designed light steel wire rope suspension bridges, with tensioned steel wire cable-supported decks. The later Abernethy suspension bridges use a design that is a hybrid of the two systems – the suspended rigid deck, which, in view of the required span, is suspended from main cables of steel wire. The pylons, transoms and finials are indistinguishable from Louis Harper's other bridges of the time. It is highly unlikely that the finial castings would have adorned these bridges had not Louis Harper been involved in their design. Certainly his son Louis R., my father, held this view in regard to the Cambus o'May bridge, saying that Louis Harper's drawings had been used, and the Aberlour one is identical.

However, although some authorities suggest that Louis Harper was involved in the other two Deeside bridges, namely at Polhollick at Ballater and the Garbh Allt Shiel Bridge near Invercauld, the evidence is less strong. The earlier bridge is that at Polhollick, built in 1892, when Louis' current design involved the tubular mast with finials. Polhollick and Garbh Allt Shiel have neither. However, Harpers was the local firm with the expertise in the cable form. Because of this uncertainty, all four

77. The bridge at Newquay as it originally appeared. (*University of Aberdeen George Washington Wilson Collections*)

THE ISLAND SUSPENSION BRIDGE. 20,994. G.W.W.

of the steel wire suspension bridges of Abernethy built in north-east Scotland are included in this account.

RIVER DEE, CAMBUS O'MAY, ABERDEENSHIRE

A young Ballater boy named Alexander Gordon had the unpleasant experience of witnessing a drowning accident in the Aberdeenshire Dee. He went home to his mother and said, 'If ever I am rich, I will build a bridge there and no one else will be drowned.' Well, this boy became a well-known London brewer, who contributed generously to several philanthropic causes in Ballater. On his death he left a sum of money

which built the Polhollick bridge and, after a space of thirteen years, the Cambus o'May bridge also.

One of the problems that led to the delay in the building of the Cambus o'May bridge was the proximity of the railway to any anchorage on that side. This was overcome by the inclusion of a 'bridge of approach' over the railway and a financial contribution by the GNSR.

There were five parties with an interest in the bridge: Lieutenant Colonel Innes of Learney (the Gordon bequest), GNSR, Mr Ean Cecil, of Glentanar, Mr Barclay Harvey of Dinnet and the Parish Council of Glenmuick (which was to maintain the bridge).

As well as being an attractive structure, the bridge was intended to allow children from the north to access their school on the south side

78. The original bridge over the River Dee at Cambus o'May in Aberdeenshire, with the bridge of approach over the Deeside railway line in the foreground. *(George Dey, Leopard Magazine, and Aberdeen Central Library)*

79. The Cambus o'May bridge after its refurbishment in 1985, when the bridge of approach over the railway on the nearer side was removed and the approach was directly from the old trackbed. *(Peter Duffus)*

without the need for a ferry, while people from the south would be able to reach the railway station on the north side. It was the twenty-second Dee crossing at that time, with a span of 164ft (15.24m).

The local authority carried out a major refurbishment of the bridge in 1985. The bridge of approach was removed and the new trussed deck now extends to the old railway line bed, now a walkway (NO420976).

RIVER SPEY, ABERLOUR, MORAY

The same Harper features are seen in the Victoria footbridge at Aberlour, nicknamed the 'penny bridge' from a longstanding toll. Today it links Aberlour with Wester Elchies on the Spey with a span of 287ft (87.48m), Abernethy's longest span. The bridge was built by Abernethy Foundry,

80. The bridge over the River Spey at Aberlour, Banffshire. (Janette Harper)

81. The Polhollick bridge over the River Dee, west of Ballater, Aberdeenshire.

Aberdeen. Wester Elchies Estate was owned at the time by a descendant of Robert Grant, a local man who had bought the estate in 1786 from Sir Archibald Grant of Monymusk.

The white lattice steel masts of the Abernethy suspension footbridges on Deeside and Speyside are well-known landmarks, but may represent the last such bridges to have been built by the company, confirming the decline in the use of this kind of bridge.

RIVER DEE, POLHOLLICK, BALLATER, ABERDEENSHIRE

The Polhollick bridge, the first to be built with funds from the Alexander Gordon bequest, is of 180ft (54.86m) span, situated a mile upstream of Ballater and was erected in 1892 by James Abernethy & Co.

The transverse links between the catenaries may have been intended to counteract the effects of wind.

RIVER DEE, GARBH ALLT SHIEL BRIDGE, ABERDEENSHIRE

This bridge, a copy of the one at Polhollick, was built by the Balmoral Estate and lies a mile downstream of the old bridge at Invercauld. It has exactly the same dimensions as the Polhollick bridge. Any Harper connection with this bridge depends on Louis' possible involvement in the Polhollick bridge of 1892 as he was no longer in active practice when the Garbh Allt Shiel bridge was built (although he is known to have remained in touch with Wyness of Abernethys professionally for a further ten years).

Louis Harper can legitimately lay claim to having been involved to a major degree in the design of the Cambus o'May and Aberlour bridges. The most significant contribution of the Harpers and their foot suspension bridges was not at home, however, but in the wider world.

82. The towers at Aberlour.

83. Garbh Allt Shiel Bridge over the River Dee, at Invercauld, Aberdeenshire.

7

TO ALL FIVE CONTINENTS

Look at this bridge suspended like a beautiful Thing of the air over the
murderous river which year after year in its flood time has devoured
its victims, men, women and children. Now there is safety for all.
(Sir W.E. Stanford, 10 September,1898)

In the second half of the nineteenth century, the British Empire was booming. In earlier times it had thrust in three directions, to North America and the West Indies, to Asia and Africa and to Australasia in the east and south, eventually covering a third of the earth's surface and embracing a quarter of its population. Following the American War of Independence, trade was soon resumed to the USA, while that to the West Indies and Canada declined. The Scottish influence in these countries was mainly through emigration, true of all the UK home countries, but the greater proportion of emigrants was Scots. In Africa and Asia in particular, the Scots diaspora had great influence in both administration and trade, but its genesis was different. The younger sons of landed families often sought their fortune abroad and many young sons of middle-class families followed them. Careers in tea, coffee and rubber were not uncommon right up to the 1950s. The developing countries were able to export to the UK commodities such as wheat, cotton, tobacco, sugar, flax, wool, tea, coffee and rubber, and in return Britain supplied manufactured goods and investment capital. From the very start of the Industrial Revolution in the UK, Britain had pulled ahead of the game, exporting 45 per cent of the world's industrial output by 1840.[41]

Thus, by 1850, strong trade links between Scotland and the developing world, including the countries of the Empire, had been established. This was just as true of north-east Scotland as elsewhere. The Aberdeen foundry William McKinnon & Co. made machinery for coffee and sugar plantations, and, in common with other foundries, such as J.M. Henderson and Barry Henry & Cook, exported 90 per cent of its output. It was little wonder that Harpers would exploit those local connections and distant markets, particularly in those countries with a non-existent industrial base and nascent infrastructure. First came their fencing and later, products from their foundries, including suspension bridges.

The Harper suspension bridge really came into its own in the developing world. Through the press reports about bridge openings at Holme and Monymusk in the 1870s, we learn that from the very start of Harpers' bridge building, exports abroad were important and a main driver of bridge development. 'Kit-built' was not a concept known to Victorians, but that is what they were. Each bridge played a major part in the development of its area and the safety of the population. The Harper bridge in the early days consisted only of the wire for the cables and hangers, together with the requisite number of cable tensioners, because the masts and deck could be constructed of timber sourced locally. The local engineer or administrator would be asked to make specific measurements of the distance required between the masts, the ordinary and flood heights of the river to be spanned, and the state and level of its banks (Appendix 2). The bridge would then be designed and the individual components manufactured. Depending on the client's wishes, the pylons, for example, could be dispatched complete or in parts. Six weeks after the company's receipt of the order, the bridge would be dispatched from the foundry by rail to the ports of Aberdeen, Liverpool, Glasgow or Southampton, from where the components were transported by ship. It was assumed that the workers who would erect the bridge on site would possess only a minimum of engineering expertise and it is unlikely that any staff from the foundry actually went out to any overseas location. More often, however, a local civil or military engineer was responsible for the erection of the bridge. By Louis Harper's time, the bridges were more sophisticated: they included lattice steel masts and adjustable anchorages, and their main cables were longer and so heavier. From the port of entry, the components would be taken, probably by mule cart or by porters on foot, to the bridge site, almost invariably a river. The distances were often considerable and the tracks poor.

Louis Harper published a general description of his bridge in 1898, which served in part as an advertisement, in part as a specification, and in part as guidance for the engineer at the site at which the bridge was to be erected. It stated that the foundation anchor blocks were of cement concrete, in which were embedded the rails and eye rods for attachment of the main ropes. The cables were of galvanised steel wire and included a core of wire to prevent elongation after erection. Special castings were secured at the rope ends, through which the limbs of the strainer adjusting screw were inserted (See Figure 28 on page 44), the whole being attached to the embedded eye rod of the anchorage.

The four pillars of the bridge were constructed of open steel latticework and set on stone or concrete. The pillars in each pair were connected to one another near the top by latticework – each pillar was surmounted by a cast-iron saddle and 'neat' finial. Individual pillars could be manufactured and transported as complete items or as a set of components. The vertical rods or hangers were of galvanised steel spaced 2ft (0.61m) apart, secured to the catenary and platform cables by special clips. The length of each rod was calculated to an accuracy of 1/16in (1.59mm) so that each might bear its own load, thus preserving the 'true dip and camber' (i.e. the sag of the catenary and the arch of the deck, respectively). The flooring consisted of timber cross-bearers, which varied in thickness according to the width of the footway. These rested on and were secured to the platform cables by hook bolts. The flooring, preferably tongued and grooved, was laid down longitudinally and nailed to the cross-bearers. Skirting was then run along either side of the platform. The sides of the bridge were guarded with strong, corrugated, diamond-wire panelling, which was secured to the vertical rods, skirting and pillars. Louis advised that the bridge be tightened by means of staple screws at eight different points (four for the main cables and four for the platform or deck cables) so that the bridge was rendered virtually rigid. The deck had a camber or arch that varied in height from 12in to 5ft, according to the span. In Louis' opinion, '…the strength of the bridge is undoubted, as it will bear a load on the platform of 160lb/sq ft, or equal to about twice the weight of all the people who could stand on it at one time.' Louis Harper's bridges were all designed to spans of multiples of 10ft (3.05m) reflecting in part the invariable hanger interval of 2ft (0.61m).

Louis Harper's agent in Bombay was a Mr Arthur Hoare, AMICE, of Turner, Hoare & Co., who published a pamphlet recommending the erection of Harpers' suspension bridges in India. After describing the bridge according to Louis Harper's specification, Hoare went on to describe just how straightforward its erection could be. This fascinating account is reproduced in full in Appendix 3. Press cuttings from the 1870s make reference to bridges having been already exported to Africa, Ceylon, Australia, India and the West Indies. These would have been of the basic design, dependent upon cable tensioners and local timber. Later, bridges were exported to parts of Africa, India, Nepal, the Falkland Islands and Estonia. With the possible exception of the bridge that was sent to the Falklands, all of these would have had lattice steel masts.

INDIA

The Public Works Department in India was founded in 1850 by Lord Dalhousie, Viceroy of India from 1848 to 1856, to advance the development of roads, railways and canals in British India.[14] Amongst its projects were the Ganges Canal and the Great Indian Peninsula Railway (GIPR). The GIPR was a 'guaranteed' railway, which meant that it was constructed and operated by a private UK company, the share capital of which was underwritten by the Indian Government. All of the eight major railway lines of the time were supported in this way.

Construction of the GIPR started in 1853, in Bombay, from which one arm extended north-east to Jabalpur and included a branch line to Nagpur, and another line ran south-east to Raichur on the Madras Railway[42]. Harpers, founded in 1856, succeeded in contracting for the fencing of the Nagpur extension and perhaps for other sections. The cast posts with integral strainers were founded at the Mealmarket Street works in around 1860 and shipped by sea from Aberdeen. This, and other Indian contracts, underpinned the Harpers' business for many years, together with similar work at home for the developing GNSR railway system. No doubt Harpers' Indian fencing connections encouraged the company to quote for bridge contracts in the same part of the world. Harpers' suspension bridges are known to have been imported to India by 1879, probably between 1871 and 1879.

In 1883 the Great Calcutta Exhibition took place. Harpers pursued its Indian interest by taking a space and entering a model Harper bridge as a promotion. It is illustrated here and is now part of the collection at Aberdeen Museum. The model bridge (the lost bridge mentioned in the Introduction) shows the basic Harper design of the time – it is similar to that of the Monymusk and Burnhervie bridges on the River Don in Aberdeenshire. Just how many of these basic bridges of John Harper were built and exactly where in India they were built is unknown.

However, we know more about the more recent bridges of Louis Harper, which had full main cables and steel lattice masts and, as often as not, a Victorian photographer available to record their opening.

We knew of three of Louis' suspension bridges built in India, from the archive photographs but locating their exact sites was challenging. In addition, two others were referred to in testimonials.

Bombay (Mumbai)

This bridge (Figure 86) was erected 'near Bombay' in 1896 under the supervision of Arthur Hoare. Arthur Hoare was a senior partner in Messrs Turner, Hoare & Co., Engineers and Contractors, Bombay and before that was head of the engineering department of John Fleming & Co. Engineers and Contractors, Bombay. Previously, he had held several posts in the railways of India and Siam.

84. Model bridge made for the 1883 Calcutta Exhibition. The cable tensioners at the mast heads are clearly visible, those at the foot only partially. (*Aberdeen Art Gallery & Museums Collections*)

85. Bridge erected near Bombay (Mumbai). (*Aberdeen Art Gallery & Museums Collections*)

86. The second bridge erected by Turner, Hoare & Co. Ltd, Bombay, at Baroda. With a span of 300ft (91.44m) and a width of 8ft (2.44m), this is the largest Harper bridge on record. (*Aberdeen Art Gallery & Museums Collections*)

The Bombay bridge appears to have been built in parkland; the photograph in Figure 85 was used extensively in the company's promotional literature. It really looks a splendid bridge. Its span measured 210ft (64.01m) and its width 6ft (1.83m). Searches of the 1in:1 mile maps of 1913 failed to identify likely footbridges, let alone a suspension bridge. The burgeoning development of Mumbai over the last century may well have eradicated the landscape in which the bridge was set in 1896. We were unable to establish whether it is still in use, despite extensive enquiries.

At the time Louis Harper wrote:

Mr Arthur Hoare, AMICE, of Messrs Turner, Hoare & Co., Engineers, Bombay, who superintended the erection, has just ordered three more Bridges and states 'that he is satisfied that for the special purposes for which they are made the Bridges are quite unique'.

Baroda (Vadodara)

One of the three orders placed by Arthur Hoare was for a bridge to be erected at Baroda, north of Bombay. This bridge was to span a distance of 300ft (91.44m) possibly over the River Mahi, and to carry a deck 8ft (2.44m) wide. This second bridge was built in 1899. It was the subject of the pamphlet reproduced in part in Appendix 3 describing the erection of a Harper bridge. It makes fascinating reading. Once again, the fate of this bridge is unknown, although one source thought it had been removed in the 1970s.

Jaidhari, Western Jumna Canal, India

In the northern plains of India, in the basin of the great Ganges, there are many irrigation canal systems, one of the most impressive being the

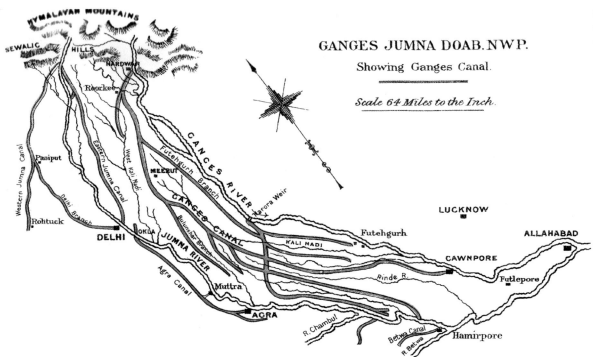

87. An outline of the Ganges canal system with the Western Jumna Canal shown on the left margin.

Jumna (Yumana) Canals – Western and Eastern. Firuz Tughlak (1351–88) undertook many public works, such as the building of dams across rivers for irrigation, tanks, caravanserais, mosques, colleges, hospitals and bridges. His greatest achievement was the old Jumna Canal. This work drew its waters from the Jumna, near a point where it leaves the mountains, and connected that river with the Ghaggar and the Sutlej by irrigation channels.[43]

In the late nineteenth century, the British restored and extended the Jumna Canal system, no doubt at the instigation of Lord Dalhousie, Viceroy of India. The Western Jumna Canal was again fully operational by 1877–78. Canal systems in India date back several centuries. Most of them were 'inundation' canals, into which water would spill if the river to which they were attached rose. As the bed of the river was often built up above the surrounding country with silt, these canals would flow to the lower ground within the river valley, the 'khadir'. However, the high

ground between water systems – the 'doab' (do = to, ab = water) was irrigated in later years by using take-off from the river at a suitably distant upstream point, so that a modest gradient from the point of egress would allow the canal to reach the doab. Thereafter, having achieved an inflow of water to the higher ground, distributing it to the land around about was straightforward.

The Western Jumna Canal followed this model, but nevertheless followed, in parts, earlier canals which were not always filled. The head of the main channel, which was 360ft (109.73m) wide, was situated on one of the numerous side streams into which the Jumna divided as it issued onto the plains from the Sewalik Mountains, a sub-Himalayan range. The water was deflected from the Jumna by weirs. The upper channel then joined the Patralla River, a tributary of the River Sombe, into which it flowed. Here, the river continued through an impressive dam, 777ft (236.83m) in width, in sixty channels, while the deflected

88. The bridge over the Western Jumna Canal at Jaidhari, 1899. (*Aberdeen Art Gallery & Museums Collections*

89. Today's Jaidhari Bridge over the Jumna (Yamuna) Canal, opened in 1942. The village of that name was situated on a narrow strip of land between the Western Canal and the Jumna River itself.

waters continued as the Western Jumna Canal near the city of Dadupur. Below this point the canal splits in two – one branch going towards Hansi and the other to Delhi, by which time its width has reduced to 120ft (36.58m). Its total length is 280 miles (451km), 243 miles (391km) of which are navigable. There are 900 miles (1448km) of distributing canals irrigating 550,000 acres (222,577ha).

Improvements to this canal system continued throughout the 1890s, towards the end of which, in 1899, the Harpers were invited to design and build a bridge over the canal. We traced the canal in the 1913 ½inch:1 mile series and found that it was possible to pinpoint the site of the bridge, about 6 miles (9.66km) from the origin of the canal, near a village also named Jaidhari, after which, presumably, the bridge was named. There appeared to be a narrow, irregular stretch of canal at the site. We visited the area in 2010, when we found that the canal had undergone considerable improvements and widening, with the construction of a

new channel to augment the flow from the River Jumna. As a result, the suspension bridge, which would have been too short at a span of 200ft (60.96m) to be of further use, was replaced in 1942 by a stone multi-arch bridge and weir.

There exists another testimonial, this time from Messrs Thos Wilson & Co., Engineers, London:

> In reply to your letter of yesterday's date, the Suspension Bridge we had from you some little time ago, 210 feet span by 6 feet wide, was duly erected by us near Bombay, and it has given much satisfaction, being greatly admired for its combination of symmetry and strength.
>
> The negative which we sent you will enable you to show this Suspension Bridge very clearly on any photograph which you may take therefrom. We should always be glad to send you any similar orders, believing that you know how to execute them thoroughly well.[39]

It is tempting to suggest that this charming testimonial refers to the bridge 'near Bombay' by Hoare, but I suspect it is another bridge, erected by another engineer, but having by chance the same dimensions. This would make five Indian bridges designed and supplied by Louis Harper.

AFRICA

John Harper was said to have exported bridges to African coffee plantations in the 1870s. At that time, Kenya would have been the principal coffee exporter in the continent. It is unlikely that these bridges could be traced today because their masts would almost certainly have perished. However, we had some information in the form of a photograph of a Louis Harper bridge in a place known in the 1870s as Transkei, and so we included this destination in a trip to South Africa in 2008.

River Tsomo, at Tsomo, Transkei, Eastern Cape

The bridge at Tsomo was built at an interesting time in the history of the Transkei. It was built for the Fingo people, a group of Xhosa who had found themselves on the losing side in the Xhosa Wars which lasted most

of the nineteenth century and had, from their origin in the high veldt, finally been driven up against the then boundary of the British Empire at the Eastern Cape. Around 1830, the Fingo sought the protection of the British Crown and were found lands within the Eastern Cape, between the border of the Eastern Cape and the Great Kei River. Later, in 1865, they were resettled a little further north in the Transkei, north of the Great Kei River, in what became known as Fingoland. Britain annexed this area as part of the deal it made with the Fingo people but also, in about 1890, made the Fingo semi-autonomous. This allowed them to raise taxes to fund community developments such as roads, schools and bridges. The Harper suspension bridge at Tsomo was one such civil engineering project initiated under this arrangement. It was 6ft (1.83m) in width and probably reached a span of about 120ft (36.58m). No doubt the colonial office in London served as intermediary between the Fingo and Harpers, but the decision to build the bridge and the authorisation of its funding belonged to the Fingo people themselves. The bridge was hailed as an example of what could be achieved by limited self-government if everybody pulled together.

90. The bridge at Tsomo, photographed perhaps during the opening speech of Sir W.E. Stanford. It is 8ft (2.44m) wide. Tsomo lies behind and the river flows from left to right. (*Aberdeen Art Gallery & Museums Collections*)

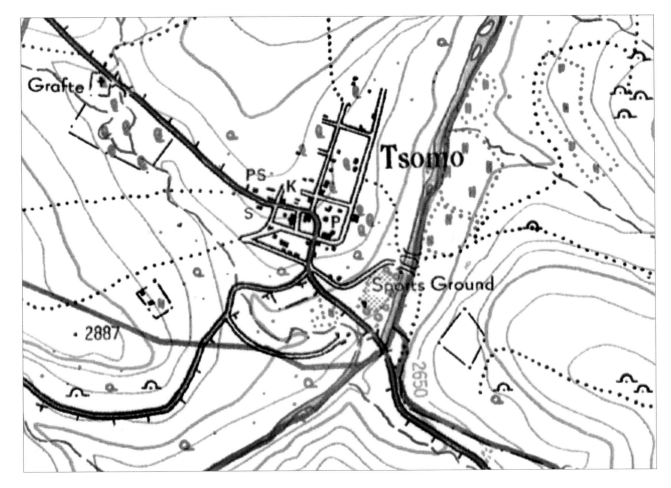

91. This map of the Tsomo area, dated 1956, shows three bridges; the present main road is shown in red and a road bridge is marked higher up. The bridge serving the footpath at the top is most likely the site of the suspension bridge. *(Chief Directorate, Surveys and Mapping, Western Cape Government, RSA)*

Referred to in the Harpers' archives as the 'Levey' Bridge, it was opened on 10 September 1898 by Sir W.E. Stanford (1850–1933), Under Secretary for Native Affairs. After outlining the recent history of the Fingo people he was addressing, Stanford concluded:

Under the wise direction of your Chief Magistrate Major Elliot, than whom no man is more loved and honoured throughout these territories! you have shown yourselves worthy of the great trust reposed in you by the Government. Look at this bridge suspended like a beautiful Thing of the air over the murderous river which year after year in its flood time has devoured its victims, men, women and children. Now there is safety for all.

The bridge is your own – built with your own money and completed without aid and direction from the Government. It is amongst the first fruits of the tree of local self-government planted in this territory by the Government. May that tree grow and flourish so that in its maturity its rich return to Fingoland will be fully recognised by all and the tears which were shed at its planting be wiped away and forgotten. God bless Fingoland.

I declare this bridge to be duly opened.

Just how underdeveloped this area was at the time can be gleaned from W.P. Livingstone's biography of Christine Forsyth,[44] a missionary of the Scots Free Presbyterian Church who, supported by the 'ladies of Greenock' established a lonely mission in 1880 at Xolobe, some 10 miles (16km) from Tsomo. Xolobe was reached by footpaths that ran through low hills covered with poor soil. According to Livingstone, medicine men reigned supreme and the only school in the area was that run by Forsyth. We had hoped to see Xolobe when we visited the area in 2008, but the road defeated us.

We drove from East London, through the pleasant rolling hills of the Eastern Cape to Tsomo, about 120 miles (193km) to the north-west. We had been given to understand that the bridge had remained in place, but this proved to be untrue. Tsomo today is a small village, a centre for the local agricultural community. It sits on high ground to the south of the river, which flows swiftly towards the Indian Ocean. At Tsomo, the river is 100ft (30.48m) wide. The 1956 map indicates three bridges – the present road bridge, another, probably older, road bridge upstream and a footbridge just above that. On the 1996 map, only the present road bridge can be seen.

We walked the banks of the Tsomo and, upstream, found the concrete footings of a road bridge, but there was no sign of the footbridge and nor did any of the locals remember it. The footbridge appears to have survived alongside an earlier road bridge and the present road bridge until some time after 1956, possibly into the 1960s. However, it was interesting to see a community that had once been served by a Harper bridge. Everybody was very helpful and friendly, particularly the children, who emerged from tiny round huts in immaculate school uniform.

ESTONIA

River Narva, at Krenholm

The factory of the Krenholm Manufacturing Company stands on the island of Kreenholm (which means Crow Island), next to a town of the same name. Krenholm was one of the largest textile mills in Europe.

92. The bridge at Narva, Estonia, built to allow access to the Krenholm Manufactory. (*Aberdeen Art Gallery & Museums Collections*)

93. Construction of the bridge at Narva, Estonia. **(a)** The masts are erected and guyed. **(b)** The main and deck cables are in position; the deck cross-bearers are fitted to the deck cables but the deck lies low. Men can be seen astride the main cable fixing the upper ends of the suspender wire or hangers at the mid point and the finials are fitted. **(c)** The deck has been raised first at its mid point to create the arch or camber; others are hanging free, ready to be connected to the deck cable. **(d)** The deck cable passing to the anchorage can be seen in the foreground. The anchorages are clearly visible and the staple screw can be seen receiving the main cable by way of the cast block. (*Aberdeen Art Gallery & Museums Collections*)

It was founded by Baron Ludwig Knoop in 1857 and designed on a principle of integrated social and aesthetic organisation – it was the site of a significant strike in 1872. The company was privatised in 1994 and came under Swedish ownership. This lasted until 2010, when it became insolvent. It continues to operate at the site in a much reduced capacity. The bridge, designed by Louis Harper to cross the water between the island and the mainland town in 1908, allowed employees to access the works. It spanned a distance of 260ft (79.25m) and measured 6ft (1.83m) in width. My father, Louis, visited the bridge in 1921, during a spell as a radio officer on a Russian icebreaker in the nearby Baltic.

I had some difficulty establishing the fate of this bridge, and letters and emails to the Krenholm Factory and the Narva Museum brought no reply. Eventually, I contacted the local authority by telephone and spoke to Julija Maltseva, who spoke good English. Several calls and emails followed, until she eventually sent me photographs from the Narva Museum, one of which is seen in Figure 92. So we were certainly talking about the same bridge. The receptionist confirmed the bridge had been destroyed during the Second World War and added that the water over which the bridge had been built had since been filled in.

These are illustrations from a unique set of fourteen photographs within the Harper archive maintained by Aberdeen Art Gallery and Museums (AAGM) and depicting the stages of bridge erection. This is the only Harper bridge to have been exported to the European mainland so far identified; was it the only one?

THE MISSING BRIDGES

We have some evidence of bridges having been ordered or sent to Australia, Ceylon (Sri Lanka), the West Indies and the Falkland Islands but unfortunately no information about their sites or present status. Many of John Harper's wooden masted bridges would not have survived long in the tropics and few would survive fifty years. Press reports in 1879 mention two bridges sent out to Australia.

By the latter part of the nineteenth century, Australia was booming – in the 1880s it had the fastest-growing economy and the highest per capita income in the world. Scottish emigrants were active in business education,

religion and farming – almost 40 per cent of Australia's borrowed capital was sourced from Scottish banks.[45]

Europe retained its place at the centre of design technology but the great distance between Europe and this developing continent, especially as a source of materials – mainly cast iron – was clearly an issue. Australian bridge builders had to rely on their own resourcefulness to counter their isolation, distance from Europe and the unique environment in which they found themselves. In particular, their projects were subject to extreme variability in river volume, which might range from dry to flood conditions, and the particular challenges that posed. When bridge builders were inhibited by large rivers, gorges and estuaries, the expansion of the European settlement was contained and development was slow.

Press reports of the opening of the bridge at Monymusk in 1879 alluded to Harpers' current engagement in the supply of two bridges to Australia. These would have been the simple tensioner-and-cable bridges, the construction of which depended on local wood for the masts and deck. I could find no information about these bridges, but I did find a clue right under my nose.

On my desk, I keep a handsome pair of brass compasses that bear the inscription, 'To J. Harper from J. Dunn, Sydney'. Recently, I came across a letter dated 1883 from James Dunn, an iron merchant of Circular Quay, Sydney to John and Margaret Harper, in which he gave family news and told of his three present bridge contracts for the Australian Government, none of which were suspension bridges. He also wrote that he had 'repeatedly offered to erect one of your wire bridges … but without effect'. It is therefore likely that James Dunn acted as agent for Harpers in Australia, although we do not know how successful he was. John Harper had mentioned Australia four years earlier at Monymusk. There are no other references to any exports by Louis Harper to Australia.

I spent some time at the State Library in Sydney trying to trace James Dunn, but without success. I also made contact with Professor Colin O'Connor of the University of Brisbane, who is regarded as the leading authority on Australia's historic bridges, but he was unaware of any Harper bridges. We need someone to come across some discarded Harper tensioner casting and then to become curious about its origins.

Again, we know from press reports on the opening of the Holme footbridge over the GNR in about 1877, that bridges were sent out to estates in Sri Lanka in the 1870s, but no traces of these bridges survive. Aberdeen had particularly strong ties with sugar, tea and rubber plantations overseas, many of which were run by Aberdonians, who would return to the north-east of Scotland on leave and would eventually retire there. There is little doubt that the facility and economy of Harpers' bridges became well known in these circles. The press report on the opening of the Newquay bridge around 1900 alludes to the construction of bridges designed by Louis in 'Cape Colony, the West Indies and Ireland'. Business cards of the time confirm that Louis built bridges in the West Indies. However, contact with the Department of Civil Engineering in the University of the West Indies has failed as yet to yield information.

Louis Harper received the following testimonial from John Birch & Co. Ltd, Engineers, London, suggesting that Harpers had supplied more than one bridge to the West Indies:

> We learn that the last bridge, of 110 feet span, which you supplied us with for the West Indies, is satisfactorily erected, and looks very well. Our client thinks that it is amply rigid, and makes no complaint of any kind. We have been promised a photograph shortly, if they have an opportunity of taking one.[39]

It's a pity the photograph has not turned up. These would have been lattice steel-masted bridges and would have survived until recent times at least.

I have had much help in my attempts to trace the Darwin Harbour bridge in the Falkland Islands from the local Department of Highways and the Stanley Museum, without success. Louis Harper mentioned this bridge in his application to become an associate member of the Institution of Civil Engineers. The Stanley Museum kindly sent me a photograph of a truss pier-supported bridge stretching across a section of the harbour that dates from 1910. I can only surmise that the Harper suspension bridge must have preceded it – between about 1890 to 1910. The bridge may have been overcome by the weather, despite its system of suspension. At nearby Goose Green there is a now-decayed, but once

handsome, suspension footbridge of 400ft (121.92m) span that was built in the 1920s by Rowell of London.

Although our investigations took us across the globe in many directions in search of Harper bridges, it became clear that the Indian subcontinent, particularly Nepal, represented the most frequent destination of the Harpers' ingenuity.

94. Trestle bridge of 1910 at Darwin Harbour, Falkland Islands. (*Stanley Museum*)

8

RIVER AND RAVINE

Nepal is not divided by its mountains but by its rivers.

(*Nepal Times*, 2002)

The climax of our travels in search of the family's bridge-building heritage was our trip to the proudly independent mountain state of Nepal in 2010. We were fairly sure that Harper bridges had remained in use until very recent years and we very much wanted to know whether any of them were still crossable.

Nepal has been described as a country divided by rivers rather than mountains. When the Swiss geologist Toni Hagen was walking in Nepal fifty years ago, he would ask villagers what they wanted most – a school, a health post or a road? The answer all over Nepal was the same, 'We want a bridge.' The usual method of crossing these often torrential waterways involved the use of single, home-made cables, negotiated hand over hand with ankles crossed above the rope and any load carried on the abdomen. The few bridges built before 1900 consisted of primitive decks laid on parallel rope cables. Professor Sylvian Levi, who travelled widely in Nepal, quoted by Percival Landon, reports a comment made in the 1600s by a Father Marc, who described crossing the torrents as so terrifying that 'travellers were blindfolded and bound to a plank, which is slung to the cables and manoeuvred across by a local expert'.[46]

In 1995, through a friend of friends, who worked at the British Embassy, I received the following email from Kamalmani Dixit, an elderly resident of Kathmandu, 'Chandra Shumshere, the Maharaja, built about two dozen bridges across Nepal – inside the Kathmandu valley as at many far flung places. All these bridges were imported from Britain.' Dixit had crossed over half a dozen of them.

Bir Shumshere, Chandra's elder brother, who died in 1901, was a member of the ruling prime ministerial dynasty of the Ranas. They ran the country for 100 years in parallel with the monarchy which was, to all intents and purposes, a constitutional body. Bir Shumshere did much to improve material conditions in Nepal in many ways. Education, hospitals, sanitary and other social services all received his special attention. Perhaps most importantly of all, he ensured the provision of a good supply of drinking water to the towns of the Kathmandu valley.[47] In all of this Bir Shumshere was ably assisted by his brother Chandra Maharaja. (The title 'Maharaja' is applied to the hereditary prime ministers of Nepal.) Bir Shumshere died in 1901 and was succeeded by his brother Deva Shumshere. After three unsatisfactory months, Deva was replaced by Chandra Shumshere. Chandra took a great interest in education, and was responsible for abolishing slavery in Nepal (1924) and outlawing the practice of *sata* (the burning alive of a widow upon her husband's funeral pyre). In 1914, Chandra placed the whole of the military resources of Nepal at the disposal of the British Government, thus initiating the origin of what would become the Ghurkha Regiment, initially part of the Indian Army.[47] However, during the Rana regime, which lasted from 1846 until 1942, Nepal remained a closed country to which few foreigners gained access. For example, although Mount Everest was known to be the highest mountain on earth, only in 1903 did a surveyor from the Indian Survey manage to enter Nepal to see Everest for himself from its foothills. The successful 1953 Everest expedition travelled on foot for three weeks from Kathmandu to reach base camp, just six years after the first expedition had been allowed access.

We have three main lines of evidence about early suspension bridges in Nepal. Firstly, our email from Kamalmani Dixit, which informed us that there had been at least three bridges on the way out of the Kathmandu Valley, at Marku and Kulekhani, all of which were suspension bridges.

96. Maharaja Chandra Shumshere.

Other bridges at Khokana and Chobhar were still intact. The Trishuli bridge in the present-day Nawakot district had been very famous, but had been demolished to make way for a road bridge in the 1970s. All of these were British bridges.

Our second line of evidence derived from Percival Landon, who had travelled extensively in Nepal in the early 1920s and had condensed his experiences into a two-volume account of the history, culture and development of the nation. In it, Landon describes the infrastructure of his day, including wire rope suspension bridges:[48]

> Wire rope suspension bridges have been thrown across the Bagmati at Chobhar★★; three over the Sun Koshi; and others over the Indrani and the Budhi Gandak at Arhunghat and the Bagmati at Sundarighat★★ and Khokna★; elsewhere the same work has been carried on across the Kali at Ridi on the main road from Palpa to Gulmi and at Ramdighat on the road from Palpa to the Valley; over the Gandak at Trishuli★★; across the Ankhu+, the Rosi★★, the Likhu★★ and the Tamor at Dhankuta; over the Marsiangti+ [sic], and at Dolka over the Lisankhu. Similar bridges have also been constructed at Cahpay, at Darandhay, at Tadi★, at Palpa on the Dhobam road and at Pangretar.

> [Author's annotation: ★★definite Harper bridges; ★probable Harper bridges; +possible Harper bridges.]

Most of these sites can be identified on the first edition map of Nepal (1in:2 miles, 1925–33).

Thirdly, a testimonial written in late 1900 by the man who erected the Harper bridges tells us of seven bridges sent out by Louis Harper to Nepal, but unfortunately not of their locations.

Colonel Kumar Nur Singh Rana, Assoc. Inst. CE, Superintending Engineer, Government of Nepal, India, wrote to Louis Harper:

> I have the pleasure to inform you that I have forwarded photo, which might be of interest to you, of one of the Bridges – 120 feet span x 4 feet wide – over the Trishuli River, which I myself erected and opened for traffic. Other bridges, 230 feet, 110 feet, 150 feet, and 90 feet by 4 feet wide, supplied by you are under construction, which I hope will be opened for traffic by next January. Everybody concerned is greatly satisfied with the rigidity, strength, neat

appearance, and the time taken for erection. Personally, I am very much pleased with the Bridge, and would not like to see any other erected, except yours. I am going to place an order for two more bridges of 180 feet and 130 feet span x 4 feet wide, and I hope to place orders for more in the future.

Louis Harper had printed below:

It may be mentioned that since the receipt of above, those 2 Bridges have been executed and dispatched, making in all 7 Bridges supplied to the Nepal Government within 2 years.

This information came to light only recently. I found it while emptying a bookcase in my mother's house, after our trip to Nepal, but it is crucial. I shall refer to the bridges Louis mentions as 'the first seven bridges'. We will return to them later.

The 1925 map by the Indian Survey allowed me to identify footbridges of that date but did not discriminate between suspension bridges and other footbridges. Other sources included photographs from friends who had come across bridges and, of course, the photographs of three bridges (all labelled 'Trishuli') in the Harper archive of the AAGM collection. I was also aware of two other bridges near Kathmandu. In all, I had some information on five different Harper bridges. What I needed was a government contact before we went out, but time was running short.

At a chance meeting at a lunch at the Royal College of Surgeons of Edinburgh a month before our departure, I met an old friend named Mike Henderson, formerly a surgeon at Dumfries and Galloway Royal Infirmary. On hearing I was going to Nepal, Mike encouraged me to make contact with a friend of his, a Professor Manohar Shrestha, Professor of Surgery at Kathmandu University. This I did and we duly met up on our first evening in Kathmandu. Professor Shrestha's brother, a civil engineer, had advised him on whom to approach and he had arranged for us to meet the head of the Nepalese Trail Bridge Support Unit (TBSU) the following afternoon.

So, within twenty-four hours of arriving in Nepal, we had the good fortune to meet our key contact. Dr Santan Arjyal, of the TBSU, was interested to hear of our quest and promised to help us in any way he could. He handed us a bridge register that contained details of all 4,000 footbridges, including suspension bridges, registered with his unit, each

97. The author and his wife Janette, with Dr Santan Arjyal of the Trail Bridge Support Unit.

marked on the map with a registration number. We couldn't believe our eyes and spent the rest of that day and all of the next extracting the information we required. As well as giving details of each bridge's name, site, district, span, river crossed and communities served, the register also gave its 'date built'. However, this was sometimes difficult to interpret;

bridges we knew were built before 1914 were sometimes recorded as having been built in the 1930s. We concluded that these dates may have represented a date of refurbishment or the date of a bridge's adoption by the body that maintained it. Either way, it meant that an early date, say 1907, was likely to be the date of building, but a later date might mean something else. In addition, early bridges were styled 'Rana' bridges, which indicated they were built during the Rana era (1845–1945). Dr Arjyal made an interesting distinction between the two main categories of trail bridge which immediately rung a bell. Firstly, a *suspension* bridge was

defined as a bridge with an arched deck, towers and a catenary; a *suspended* bridge had neither and its deck was laid directly on a concave catenary. You will recall that, with reference to the system of suspension established by John Harper in the 1870s, the Harper manufactory had claimed that the principles of his unstiffened suspension bridge were 'tension, suspension and arch'. Louis Harper was responsible for all of the suspension bridges built in Nepal in the first decade of the twentieth century and it appears that all suspension bridges erected in the country since then have followed Harper's unique specification for unstiffened (i.e. with a cable-supported

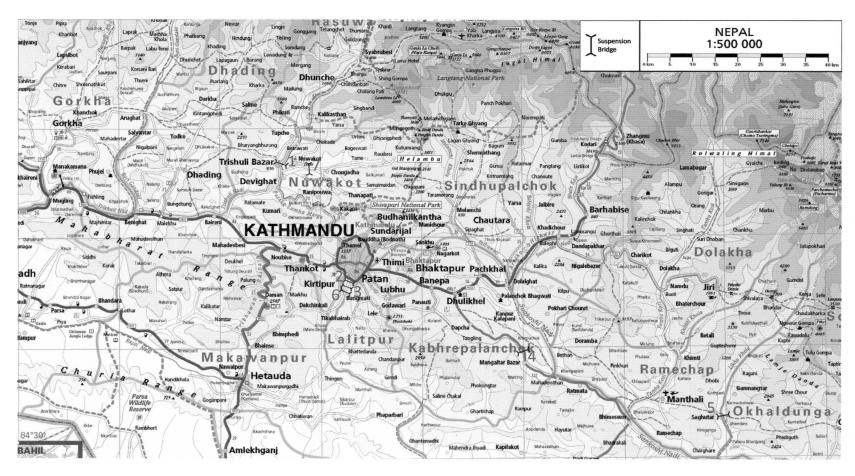

98. This map is a section of the map 'world mapping project Nepal'. *(Reise Know-How, Verlag Peter Rump GmbH)*

deck) suspension footbridges, right up to the present. Presumably, Nepalese engineers have found this configuration to give stability in the adverse climate of this mountain state, have stuck with it and have thus defined a suspension bridge as a bridge with an arched deck cable.

The TBSU is funded by the Nepalese and Swiss governments. Its function is to receive requests from local authorities for local bridges, assess these and to provide resources for completing those that are approved. Thereafter, grants towards routine maintenance to an agreed level are awarded and the TBSU takes responsibility for major works. Today, the number of trail bridges in the country totals about 4,000 and another 6,000 are under consideration.

Many of the suspension bridges in the register were categorised as belonging to the 'Rana epoch'. This, combined with the 1925 map and Kamalmani Dixit's enormously helpful email, allowed us to plan our field trips. We would concentrate on the ancient trails in central Nepal, where it is logical to assume that the earliest infrastructure would have been built. There were three areas to look at – the southern approaches to Kathmandu from India, including the valley of the Bagmati River, the Trishuli and its tributaries to the north-west (the junction of an India–Tibet route with the Gorka–Kathmandu trail) and the Sunkoshi River and its tributaries to the east (on the Kathmandu–Tibet route). Figure 98 is an up-to-date map of central Nepal covering the area of our travels. Footpaths are still prominent and the old tracks can still be discerned. However, much road building has now taken place, although often these are not much of an improvement on the old tracks.

THE HIGH ROAD FROM KATHMANDU

I was interested to see something of this ancient route into Kathmandu from the south and early one morning I left Kathmandu with our driver.

As we approached the precipitous hills that form the rim of the Kathmandu basin to the south-west, I could see neither a col nor a gap in the skyline that the road might exploit. How on earth were we going to drive up there? I soon found out as we proceeded to negotiate a road that twisted around sharp hairpin bends and crawled up incredible gradients, to the steep, forested mountainside, and suspended over massive drops to the terraces below. This road was the last section of the track connecting India and Kathmandu, now replaced by a paved road further west. I asked about the procession of Tata 4 × 4s that regularly forced us to enjoy a kind of vehicular pousette, teetering over the brink or shaving a cliff as we toiled uphill. 'To some, this is still the route to Kathmandu from India,' replied my host. It is still the most direct route, albeit not suitable for heavy traffic. Landon, writing in 1928, describes the descent of this section of the high road. He had just reached the summit of the ridge above the road on which we had been driving:

> This is the crux of the entire route. The gradients vary from thirty to over forty-five degrees in steepness. Only one corner is actually over fifty degrees, but the points are not infrequent when one descends a yard for every yard one moves forward. From time to time one meets with massive stone stair-treds, but they are worn smooth and in nearly all cases are broken and slating at angles; often it is better to use the raw side of rough rock embedded in the hillside that drops beside them. But, bad though this way is, it is of almost indescribable beauty.[49]

Even on the ascent, this was a white-knuckle ride and not for the faint-hearted, although it was no problem for our Nissan Patrol and its inscrutable driver. The Kathmandu Valley is shaped like a saucer and this route represents part of its rim. Formerly, it stood as the last line of defence against intruders and signs of the old military buildings can still be seen at the top. This 'High Road to Kathmandu' had, over centuries, seen men carry in everything that Kathmandu required from the wider world – including statues, cars (for the Maharajas to drive in the palace grounds because there were no roads anywhere else), and manufactured goods, amongst which were the components of a Harper-manufactured suspension bridge. I tried to imagine what it must have been like for the porters, burdened by their loads, to negotiate the track as it clung to the sides of small ravines. The main cables may have been slung on a pole and carried between two men; all the other components were capable of being split into smaller loads. The total weight of, say, a 300ft (91.44m) span bridge would have been 12.65 tons (12,852kg) and its heaviest component would have weighed 500lb (227kg). In 1925, long after the Harper suspension bridges had been built, the transportation of

99. Hydro scheme at Kulekhani/Marku. How many bridges lie beneath?

goods was improved by the establishment on this section of a 14-mile electrically driven ropeway,[50] which dropped to its northern terminus at Kisipidi (Thankot), near Kathmandu. During the course of its 14 miles, the two passes crossed important aspects of the defence of Kathmandu and, therefore, passengers were still compelled to walk!

From the summit of the Chandragiri Pass we had just scaled, we had a wide view to the south-west over broad terraces on which maize, rice, millet and colourful mustard grew. This area, which lies close to Chitlang, is one of relatively prosperous agriculture in which the manufacture of goat's cheese represents an important local industry, and is in complete contrast to the north-facing slope we had just scaled. We followed the line of the old ropeway down towards Marku and Kulekhani and could see people still using the original footpath etched into the hillside.

We soon reached Marku, which was mentioned in Kamalmani Dixit's email as the site of an early British bridge. However, the 1925 map made no mention of a bridge at this site and thus we assumed that the most likely possibility was that a later bridge had been erected there, perhaps by Henderson. John M. Henderson Ltd was established in Aberdeen in 1866 and by 1900 was described as a business comprising consulting engineers, machine and cranemakers, covering a site of 4 acres (1.6ha) between King Street and West North Street – it is now occupied by a supermarket. The firm continues today in Arbroath. It achieved a considerable reputation worldwide for its production of cranes, overhead cableways and drag lines. In 1929, the company erected five great cableways over the River Nile at Nag Hammadi, in Egypt, in connection with the barrage there. Each cableway was 3,100ft (944.88m) in length, supported by towers 182ft (55.47m) in height – the largest in the world at the time. Like Harpers, Hendersons were later to build several foot suspension bridges in Nepal.

As we approached Marku, we realised that it was likely that we would never know the location of any bridges because the whole area had been flooded by a hydro scheme. A local man told us that four bridges remained under the water and became quite excited, jabbing his forefingers in the air when he saw my photograph of a Harper bridge with its finials. He also explained in sign language that the submerged bridges had wooden decks, unlike the steel grid decks of the modern footbridges. Kamalmani Dixit had suggested there were three in this area and how many of the local man's four were suspension or suspended bridges could not be clarified. To the south, this hydro scheme includes a dam at Kulekhani, where there was certainly a bridge by 1925 – one is shown on the map of that year. This was one of Dixit's British bridges, standing at the southern end of the famous ropeway, although it is not mentioned in Landon's list of wire suspension bridges.[48]

Logically, it is likely that this would have been a Harper bridge, situated as it was on the India–Kathmandu route around 1900. A bridge at this key position would have facilitated the building of all subsequent bridges because all of the components would have been transported this way. However, this bridge now also lies under several hundred feet of water, albeit that it is probably in perfect condition!

KOKHANI, RIVER BAGMATI

The return journey into the Kathmandu Valley took us due east from Kulekhani. Once we reached the col, we had a view of the Kathmandu basin and below to the valley of the Bagmati. Our road led down over gentle terraced slopes to Khokana, where the lowest of the three Harper bridges over this river may have been placed (see site 6, Figure 98 on page 116). Today, the bridge at Khokana is an impressive arched suspension bridge, 400ft (121.92m) in length, that was built in 1969 to replace an earlier bridge of 1903. It is unlikely that Louis Harper built bridges that exceeded 300ft (91.44m) in clear span, but it would have been possible to span this river with a much shorter bridge by using the lower ground. However, it is likely that such a site would have been vulnerable to flood and this may have been the reason for its replacement. I believe, however, that the bridge built here must have been a Harper bridge, firstly because no-one else was building bridges in Nepal at the time and, secondly, because the Harper bridge upstream was built in the same year, as was a third bridge nearer to Kathmandu. Unfortunately, we have no photograph of this 1903 bridge.

100. The Kathmandu Valley from the south, looking down to Kokhani and Chobar in the middle distance, beyond which is Kathmandu.

CHOBHAR, RIVER BAGMATI

Two kilometres upstream on the River Bagmati is the famous Chobhar Gorge, now a World Heritage Site (Site 3, Figure 98 on page 116). Legend has it that the gorge was created by the sword of the goddess Bodhisattva Manjushri in a single blow to the rock in order to drain a lake that occupied the Kathmandu Valley – there is geological evidence that there was once a lake in the valley. A Harper bridge was built here in 1903. Its erection was commemorated in a plaque that tells us the bridge, known as the Chandra Bridge, was erected by a Brigadier Colonel Kumar Nursingh Rana Badadur CE, AMICEMSA, Superintendent Engineer, Government of Nepal, Kathmandu, presumably a member of the ruling family. Like many of the family, he is likely to have been educated in Britain and no doubt received his engineering qualification there. With such a background, Rana Badadur may have been the key figure in the selection of Harper bridges to help facilitate the early development of his country, and his testimonial quoted earlier supports

this. The plaque also suggests that the army erected the early bridges. Rana Badadur also signed the photographs of the Harper bridge at Trishuli Bazar and sent them to Louis Harper in 1900. A second plaque confirms the maker's name.

The Chandra Bridge over the Chobhar Gorge is 130ft (39.62m) long and has a deck of 4ft (1.22m) in width. Its main cable is 1¼in (32mm) in diameter and the deck cables measure 1in (25mm) in diameter. The deck was wooden and remained similar to the original until the early 1990s when the bridge acquired a steel deck supported on a light, braced sub-frame which, in turn, was fixed to the original deck cables and to the steel sub-deck cross-members. The hangers now pass to the cross members positioned below the deck rather than directly to the deck cables. This modified deck arrangement had been universally applied to all the suspension and suspended bridges we encountered, apart from the odd one that was no longer maintained. They remain essentially 'unstiffened' bridges, but are made more stable by the increased deadweight of the deck. The arch is maintained.

101. The Chobar Bridge over the River Bagmati. (*Insight Guide, early 1990s*)

102. The Chandran Bridge at Chobar today with the accompanying road bridge. The deck is now steel, but the towers, cables and anchorages are original. (*Jeena Maskey*)

One of the advantages of the steel deck is that it accommodates the heavy motorcycle traffic. There are hordes of motorcycles on the roads leading to the Chandra Bridge, which makes it a little difficult for foot travellers. This is less of a problem at Chobhar than elsewhere because a few years ago a concrete road bridge was built a few metres away. Nevertheless, the cessation of activity at the nearby cement works, the fact that there is the famous temple dedicated to Jal Binayak nearby and the presence of a recently laid hill garden have all helped this spectacular gorge with its Victorian bridge to gain World Heritage Site status.

SUNDARI, RIVER BAGMATI

Just a kilometre upstream, and almost at Kathmandu, is the next Harper bridge, connecting Kirtipur in the west with Lalitpur (Patan) in the east (site 2, Figure 98 on page 116). This is the Sundari Bridge. This was our first sight on this trip of a Harper bridge of 280ft (85.34m) in span, and it looked impressive. The towers, anchorages and cables all looked original. The main cable measured 1¾in (44mm) in diameter. A deck identical to that at Chobar must have been installed in the 1990s because our photograph of that date shows wooden decks. The deck modification, to a width of 4ft (1.2m), has led to changes in the hanger and deck structures similar to those in the Chandra Bridge. In addition, at each side of the deck the bridge carries an 8in (203mm) water main, which adds to the weight and rigidity of the deck. This security of supply is much appreciated by the residents of nearby Patan.

TRISHULI RIVER SYSTEM BRIDGES

The Trishuli River lies to the north and west of Kathmandu, and is about four hours away by road. Photographs of three bridges within this river basin are maintained in the AAGM archive.

103. The Sundari bridge over the Bagmati just south of the Kathmandu ring road. (*Jeena Maskey*)

DHIKURE, RIVER TADI

Study of the 1925 maps showed only one footbridge over the River Trishuli itself, at Trishuli Bazar (Bidur) (site 1, Figure 98 on page 116). It will be recalled that we had sourced three archival photographs of bridges, all built prior to 1925. Another footbridge was located over a tributary, the Tadi, not far away at Dhikure Bazar, on the old trail from Kathmandu to Trishuli Bazar and the ancient Ghurkha town of Gorku. (Dhikure does not appear on the map in Figure 98. It lies due south of Nawakot, east of Trishuli Bazar and is site 7). This would be a logical site for a Harper bridge because there was certainly one previously at Trishili Bazar. The date given in the TBSU register for the original crossing at Dhikure was 1911.

On our way to Trishuli Bazar, we diverted to Dhikure, adding a couple of hours to our journey. We passed up the river, through a wide strath characterised by a profusion of broad rice terraces, banana plantations, bamboo and some livestock, until we reached our destination. We were directed along a narrow street that led to the river and, as we made our way towards the water, over the rooftops there came into sight a Harper finial! Rounding the corner, we found that this feature was supported by a surprisingly modern bridge. This bridge had been built in 1969, replacing a much older bridge. By the time we reached it, a small crowd had formed around us and followed us across the bridge. I showed an old man the picture of the Harper bridge and he confirmed that the original bridge had been like the bridge in the picture, complete with the finials,

104. The modern bridge over the Tadi and our first sight of the finials derived from Louis Harper's design. Is imitation the sincerest form of flattery?

which he picked out. William Brook Northey, writing in 1925, referred to 'a fine suspension bridge' over the Tadi.[47]

However, the finials on the present-day bridge were not Harper castings. Were they copies intended to recall the earlier bridge? Or did they perhaps represent a traditional decoration by virtue of their similarity to the finials seen on Hindu temples? This was not to be the only time we saw such ornaments. The present-day bridge spanned 400ft (121.9m); thus, if the previous bridge had been a Harper bridge, its approaches and abutments would have been built into the stream.

It is entirely logical that this bridge, on the route to Trishuli Bazar from Kathmandu, would have been built around the time of the bridge we were to consider next, which was erected in 1900.

TRISHULI BAZAR, RIVER TRISHULI

There was less doubt about the bridge at Trishuli Bazar (see Site 7, Figure 98 on page 116). Now a road bridge occupies the site but it was clear that the photographs in our possession were of the previous suspension bridge – the houses and slopes of the village were identifiable even today. The bridge was not in the register, presumably because the replacement was a road bridge. The photograph is signed by Kumar Nursingh Rana, the brigadier engineer who later erected the Batgami bridge at Chobhar, and is helpfully dated 1900. Colonel Rana's testimonial suggests that the bridge at Trishuli Bazar was the first Harper bridge to be completed, the other four are described as being in the course of construction. In the Harper archive, at Aberdeen Museum however, one of them is dated 1899, although this may reflect the year it was dispatched rather than the date of its erection. Rana signed the photographs in October 1900 and must have made his testimonial around the same date. Louis Harper's comment about the seven bridges supplied to the Nepalese Government in the previous two years may refer either to the period 1898–1900 or, more likely, 1899–1901.

In Figure 106, which shows the Trishuli Bridge completed, a track can be seen making an oblique ascent of the far hillside along the path that our road to Betrawati would take 100 years later.

This was an important trail, connecting as it did Kathmandu and Gorka, the cradle of Gurkha culture. Both the Tadi and Trishuli Bazar

bridges lay on this route and it is possible that another Harper bridge was built nearer to Gorka but unfortunately we didn't have time to explore this area. The Trishuli Bazar bridge illustrates another problem we had with the TBSU Register. As the suspension bridge had been replaced by a road bridge, it was not included in the register. This would also have been true of any suspension bridge removed for any reason. The TBSU document represented a current register, not a historical one. We had to rely on the detail contained in Langton's account of 1928.

Many of these sites can be identified today although, whereas the early bridges represented links in the principal trails of the early years of the twentieth century, they are now larger bridges fed by vehicular roads. Whether any signs remain in the vicinity of their suspended predecessors remains to be established. From Trishuli, we left the old east–west Kathmandu to Gorka route to join the old south–north route to Tibet. The most likely sites for the two unidentified 'Trishuli' Harper bridges are crossings over the Tadi at Dhikure and over the Marsiangti near Gorka, both of which are sites mentioned by Landon.[48] Both these could also be described as within the Trishuli area.

The road north to Batrawati is so rough that it verges on the impossible. The next 20 miles or so lay along a road in the process of being made or remade. This follows the route of an ancient high pass to Tibet and China from India – it seemed to us as if we were right behind the first bulldozer to carve a way north. In addition, several recent landslides had blocked the route and bulldozers and diggers were still trying to clear a way through. We advanced across the rubble in the hope that the landslide had slid as far as it was going to, somewhat reassured to be following a large Tata ten-wheeler full of spoil and a bus full of people, the top deck (i.e. the roof rack) of which was also crowded with passengers and luggage! I estimated the descent to the tiny river far below to be around 3,000ft (914m).

A bridge over the Betrawati River, as it enters the Trishuli at the town of the same name, is shown on the 1925 map. However, it is not marked as a footbridge but as something wider, despite the lack of roads and reliance on tracks at the time. Now somewhat derelict, having been bypassed by a road bridge, we wondered just how old this footbridge actually was (Figure 109). The register suggests 1910 but the locals estimated 1930. The latter would fit in with the cartography. The register and the 1925 map are at variance and the site does not appear on Landon's list.[48]

105. The bridge over the Trishuli River, under construction. (*Aberdeen Art Gallery & Museums Collections*)

One important piece of information was not in doubt. This bridge had been built by John M. Henderson of Aberdeen. The job number confirms the date as 1926. This is of interest in our story because the construction details of the towers were similar to those in the two Henderson bridges in Nepal, one of which we observed at Betrawati.

In Figure 110a we can see that the lateral supports of the towers are constructed of steel beams placed at an angle to the horizontal, forming a zigzag pattern up the tower. This pattern was seen in the cableways in Egypt, in a Henderson bridge over the River Tweed at Mertoun (Figure 110b) and, as we were to find later, in the bridge over the Monohara tributary of the Batgami, at Kathmandu. I asked Allan Grattidge, formerly a director of J.M. Henderson, about the zigzag laterals. 'Well, just the same construction as our crane jibs,' he replied. So this was merely a different application for a tried and tested girder design.

We continued on along the horrendous road, which gained considerable height as we followed it further north, only to drop by multiple hairpins

107. A 4ft (1.33m) wide bridge in the Trishuli area, site not yet identified. (*Aberdeen Art Gallery & Museums Collections*)

106. The Trishuli River bridge completed. (*Aberdeen Art Gallery & Museums Collections*)

108. An early bridge, labelled 'Trishuli', site unknown. Interestingly, the width here appears to be greater than 4ft, and according to Col. Rana's testimonial, all seven bridges supplied between 1899 and 1901 were 4ft (1.33m) wide, so it may have been built later. (*Aberdeen Art Gallery & Museums Collections*)

109. The Betrawati bridge.

110. The trestle style tower and zig-zag laterals of a Henderson tower, seen at **(a)** Betrawati (1926) and **(b)** over the Tweed at Mertoun (1929).

(around which our tired driver enjoyed accelerating!) to the bailey bridge across the river to Syaphru just beyond. The headwaters above this point belong to the Bhote Koshi and the Langtang. Each of these can be crossed by a foot suspension bridge – the one over the Bhote Koshi is modern, whereas that over the Langtang is dated as constructed in 1935 in the TBSU register. The date for the erection is probably correct, but its origin remains a mystery. It bears a strong resemblance to the bridge we had seen earlier at Dhikure over the Tadi, except the latter had in addition the imitation Harper finials.

Thus, within the Trishuli river system, we identified three bridges depicted in our archive photographs and confirmed as having originated in Harpers' facility in Aberdeen. One of these preceded the present bridge at Trishuli Bazar, one may have preceded the present bridge over the River Tadi at Dhikure and the third, a smaller bridge, may have been supplied in 1899 (see Figure 108) but erected after the bridge at Trishuli Bazar. One possible site for the latter bridge is further to the west on the

111. The Langtang bridge, showing the trestle type towers and a 'boxy' saddle for the cables. Made from Scottish steel; manufacturer unknown.

approach to Gorka. It will almost certainly have been located at one of the sites mentioned by Landon.[48]

We encountered several modern trail bridges, both suspension and suspended, on our trek up into the Langtang area. The Nepalese are currently building mainly suspended bridges. The cable that supports the deck is also the catenary and the handrails are tensioned in addition. These represent a cheap and practical way of providing local communities with safe access.

Our diversion into the Langtang National Park brought us into closer contact with the local people, who were mainly of Tibetan origin. One evening, after our meal, I gave up trying to read by the light of my head-torch and simply enjoyed the smoky stove and the animated conversation of the guides and their friends around me. A small, somewhat unkempt, barefoot boy, aged maybe 7 years old, overcame his shyness and came to stand at my knee, looking at my book. He traced the embossed title with his finger and then, in impeccable English, pronounced each letter. His primary school at Langtang, at 10,000ft (3,048m) above sea level, obviously held our language in high regard. It may be that children like these are regarded as future Ghurkhas, but the incident reminded me of the close ties between Nepal and the UK that date back to the Ranas of the nineteenth century.

THE SUNKOSHI RIVER BRIDGES

The Sunkoshi is an impressive river to the east of Kathmandu (see Figure 98 on page 116) and represented our third area of search. We knew that by 1928, three steel wire suspension bridges had been erected over the Sunkoshi,[48] one of the largest rivers in Nepal to the east of Kathmandu. We travelled first to Dhulikhel, where we established ourselves at a local hotel, then continued on to look at our first bridge on the Sunkoshi, at Dolalghat, at its confluence with the Indrawati tributary. As we approached the bridge, which sits beside a modern road bridge, we saw once again that the towers were decorated with Harper-style finials, but the towers themselves were not of Harper origin. The trestle style towers on this bridge are very similar to those of both the Tadi and Langtang bridges.

All four of these Rana bridges – at Dhikure over the Tadi (see Figure 104 on page 24), at Langtang (see Figure 111 on page 130),

at Dolalghat over the Sunkoshi (see Figure 112), and near Palpa over the Dobhan, west of Kathmandu[47] – were surely built by the same company: the towers are similar, as are the saddles, and all have twinned catenaries and deck cables. All but one have imitation Harper finials. Yet, despite certain similarities they are neither Harper nor Henderson in origin. The curious point is that a similar design was used for a period of roughly fifty years from 1910 until the 1960s. This third early suspension bridge builder has yet to be identified. One candidate might be Messrs Burn & Co., the company that built the first metal suspension bridge in Afghanistan in 1909. It was not unlike the one at Dolalghat, but without the finials. Nowadays Burn Standard Company Ltd continues as a nationalised company carrying out civil engineering projects for the Indian Government.

This bridge over the Sunkoshi was registered as having been built in 1909. This is supported by the plate on the bridge, which declares:

Erected by order of His Highness the Major General Sir Chandra Shum Shere, Jung Bahadur Rana Thong-Lino-Pim-Ma-Ko-Kwang-Jang-Shang, Prime Minister. Marshall of Nepal 1909.
(N27deg 38.433 E85 deg 42.61)

It seems clear that this is the only bridge to have occupied the site. It is possible that Harpers' usual maximum span of 300ft (91.44m) was not enough for this large river. This bridge appears to be the earliest non-Harpers bridge in Nepal and spelled the end of Harpers' monopoly that had been enjoyed since 1900. Despite the presence of the road bridge, this footbridge is still maintained. That particular day it was occupied by a herd of goats, the billy butting my behind as I transgressed his territory. There was a plate celebrating its opening, but no mention of its origin or any predecessor.

Further up the Sunkoshi is a modern suspended bridge, the Lamosangu bridge, erected in 1998 by the Swiss Aid Programme. Previously, this site was home to a Henderson bridge built around 1930 and famous for having been crossed by successive Everest expeditions on their way out of Kathmandu. The original footings are still in place, and one of the tensioning screws for a deck cable could be seen in the undergrowth, suggesting a width of 3ft (0.9m).

112. The bridge over the Sunkoshi River at Dolalghat, by an unknown builder.

We returned to Dhulikhel and our hotel for the night. The next day, we were to visit one of two bridges from 1907 – one on the Roshi tributary of the Sunkoshi. The second bridge, over the Likhu, was too remote for us to see in the time we had available.

MANGALTAR, RIVER ROSI

Staying at the hotel was an American called Peter Owens. He had heard we were Scots and stopped us as we left the car park to tell us that there were two bridges near Kathmandu that had been manufactured in Scotland. Yes, I replied, I knew of them, adding that they had been built by my grandfather. Owens was lost for words. I told him we were hoping to see another one at Mangaltar and he said that his party was going that way too and would meet us there.

The road to Mangaltar, heading south-east, is a new one built by the Japanese and it represents a welcome change from the roads in the west.

113. **(a)** The modern suspended bridge at Lamosangu and **(b)** its suspension predecessor by J.M. Henderson.

114. The footings of the original Henderson bridge at Lamosangu.

115. The Harper foot suspension bridge at Mangaltar on the Roshi River, a tributary of the Sunkoshi.

Accordingly, we covered the 20 miles quite quickly and soon arrived at our bridge, situated in a gorge of the Roshi River, a tributary of the Sunkoshi.

After all our travelling and all the disappointment that accrued whenever we found we were too late to see a Harper bridge *in situ*, here at last was the real thing, located by our search strategy rather than through someone else's previous sighting or published description. The bridge was unmistakably a Harper product and at 130ft (39.62m), it was of modest span, but it represented a real gem. It bore no plate and its deck had been recently modified, but its cables, anchorages and masts were original and it looked very well maintained.

SANGATUR, RIVER LIKHU

Back on the road, we were joined by Peter Owens and his party, all of whom were equally excited by our find. With them was a local Nepali man, Kalu Tamang. He told us that he had been brought up in the village of Mukpa, not far away on the other side of the bridge and so had known it all his life. He said that if we were to walk due east along a track for two days, we would come to an identical bridge, still in use. Out came the maps and Kalu Tamang identified the bridge over the Likhu River at Sanghutar, built in the same year, 1907. We were left in no doubt that this remote bridge

116. The Harper bridge at Singultar on the Likhu tributary of the Sunkoshi. (*Nirmal Raj Joshi*)

represented the fourth Harper bridge to remain in use today in Nepal (confirmed by examination of this image). So ended a day of highlights.

Our search in Nepal suggests that the Harpers built the earliest known suspension bridge of modern times in that country, somewhere in the basin in around 1900, and thereafter built all of the suspension bridges to be constructed in Nepal in the following decade. Seven had been built or supplied by 1900 – these may or may not have included the three over the Batgami, which we know date from around 1903. Matching their spans with those of the bridges on the list of the first seven bridges shows that it is possible that one of the bridges mentioned by Louis Harper, of 130ft in span, may have been erected at Chobhar in 1903. We can speculate that the other mentioned by Louis, which had a span of 180ft (54.86m), may have been destined for Kokhani in the same year. Of the original five, the only one we can be sure about is that at Trishuli Bazar – the sites of the other four are unknown. Our two photographs of bridges 'over the Trishuli' but not over the parent stream cannot be easily reconciled with the list without further information. It is, however, likely that the bridges over the Rosi at Mangaltar and over the Likhu at Sanghutar, dated 1907, were not included within the first seven supplied seven years earlier. This is also true of the Sundari Bridge over the Batgami, upstream of Chobar. Its span of 280ft (85.34m) does not match any of the details given for the first seven, and thus it may have derived from a date later than 1903. Thus we might conclude that, in all, the Harpers may have built as many as eleven bridges in Nepal between 1900 and 1910, possibly even more. Significantly, the Nepalese today define a suspension bridge according to John Harper's original criteria of 'suspension, tension and arch', and use this format within the specification of all suspension bridges built to this day in Nepal. This is perhaps John Harper's greatest legacy.

Shortly after we arrived in Nepal, the daily newspaper *Republica* featured on its front page a photograph of a woman crossing a river torrent by means of a single cable, suspended by her hands and ankles and carrying a sack of grain across her middle. The caption to the photograph informed us that many people still crossed rivers in this way but that recently, in the same area, two young girls had been lost doing this when the cable gave way. In the last 100 years, although much has been achieved to provide safe crossings in this mountain state, much remains to be done.

117. Dodhara Chandani Bridge is an impressive, recently built, four-arch foot suspension bridge of 1.2km in western Nepal. Where did they get the idea for those cables of opposite curvature? (*Dr S. Aryjal*)

That Harpers' bridges were erected in locations across the globe emphasises the trade links between the UK and many other parts of the world and demonstrates how successfully the Harpers exploited their experience in providing fencing for railways, built on that experience and developed it, and made particular use of the links between the north-east of Scotland and the tea, coffee, sugar and rubber fraternity worldwide.

Harpers' export business worldwide between 1870 and 1910 was of considerable importance, influencing the design of components and the evolution of their light steel wire suspension footbridges. The company's influence is still in evidence in Nepal today.

9

FATHER AND SONS

Mr Harper, who has introduced and perfected a new industry in
the locality and thus afforded employment to hundreds of people,
cannot fail to have made the community deeply grateful to him.

(*The Northern Figaro*, 1886)

In this final chapter we will trace the progress of the various family branches into the twentieth century and discover how the business also extended in different directions, very much reflecting the socioeconomics of the times. It will be recalled that the brothers John and Hugh Harper left the north-east for the central belt of Scotland as teenagers, working in the fencing trade in Edinburgh and Glasgow.

On their return to Aberdeen in 1856, John, with his wife Eliza and children Lizzie and John Jnr, stayed at 87 Queen Street, right in the heart of the commercial district of the city, along with John's brother Hugh. The following year Eliza died of pulmonary tuberculosis. In 1862, John married Margaret Ross and their only child Louis was born in 1868. By this time the business was well established and prospering. Within the range of homes, a steady rise in status can be discerned as the family that had started out as artisans gradually became comfortably middle class. In confirmation of their new status, the Harpers moved out of town to the old Freedom Lands of Aberdeen, to Rubislaw. In 1872 John purchased the lands of Seafield, which extended to about 60 acres (24.2ha) which is today bounded by Seafield Road, Anderson Drive, the West Burn of Rubislaw and Viewfield Road. Seafield lies 3 miles (4.8km) from the city centre. John built three villas facing east to look across open country and the bleachfields of the textile mills towards the sea and the city, which had encroached as far as Forest Avenue. Thorn Villa (later Thornlea) was

for Hugh, Monaltrie for Peter (a blacksmith in the business) and Seafield House was intended for himself. Hugh stayed for a few years at Thorn Villa and then moved to other addresses in Aberdeen's West End, but Peter never took up the offer of Monaltrie.

A frequent visitor to Seafield was Mr George Cruickshank, an old family friend who had been clerk to Sir Alexander Anderson, a former Provost of Aberdeen after whom Anderson Drive was named. George Cruickshank later moved to a similar post with London County Council and could thus serve in *loco parentis* to young Louis during the latter's time at school in Kent. Cruickshank brought his daughters to stay with the Harpers in Aberdeen for three weeks each year. It was a matter of great fascination to the Harper grandchildren that George had an artificial leg. Each morning, as he prepared for his cold bath, the children would wait with baited breath to hear the resounding clunk that rang through the house as he hung his leg on the bathroom door – a cause of great hilarity.

John Harper had started his working life as a gardener and this showed in the beautiful policies he developed around the house, now occupied by Mayfield Gardens, where the outline of the drive can still be seen passing through the central green of that development. John and Margaret remained in Seafield House until 1904, when they moved to a newly built bungalow, immediately adjacent to the house and connected to it by a conservatory. The bungalow is now No. 9 Mayfield Gardens and

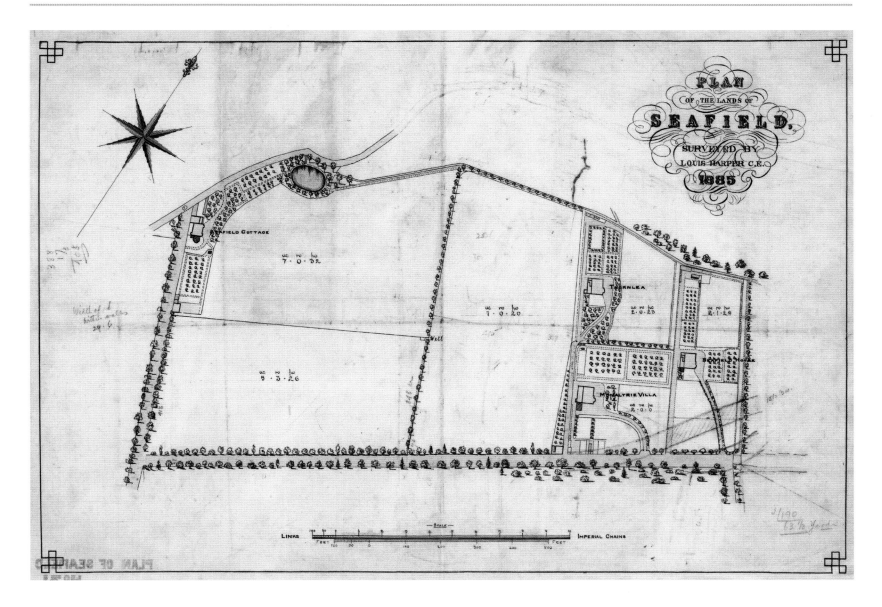

118. Louis Harper's plan of the lands of Seafield. The pencilled amendment indicates the possible lines of the link between Seafield Road and the future Anderson Drive.

Seafield House is No. 11. Margaret Harper died in 1905 and John in the following year. In 1904, John's second son, Louis, and his young family moved from their home in Gladstone Place to nearby Seafield.

After 1876, John's first son John Jnr took an increasing role in the business and became managing director, probably when Harpers Ltd was

119. Taking the work home: a temporary folly in the garden with George Cruickshank and his daughter in the background. (*Aberdeen Art Gallery & Museums Collections*)

set up in 1885. John Jnr was still heavily dependent on the advice of his father, as their correspondence in 1887 about the Nairn and Cromdale bridges illustrates. He was particularly interested in having photographs taken of the various bridges and in publishing brochures to advertise the firm. In the late 1880s he frequently informed his father that he 'would very much like to know *at once* when Louis' time is up' (with Jenkins & Marr, Architects and Civil Engineers, to whom Louis was apprenticed) 'as bridge pushing arrangements hinge a good deal on that'. He clearly thought that Louis might start his career with the family firm by taking on the editing and development of publicity and advertising. Perhaps it is to John Jnr we owe a debt of gratitude for the photographic record we have inherited. At this time, John Jnr seems to have been based in London as the firm's representative, although he also maintained Aberdeen addresses during the 1880s. A London locus was important for securing contracts throughout the Empire via government departments. Letters of the time

tell of the worry he and his wife Elizabeth had over their daughter Lizzie (b. 1882), who was very ill with rheumatic fever. It was from this time onward that John Jnr's side of the family gradually became established in London, where their descendants remain today.

By the turn of the century, John Jnr's interest was less in the foundry and more in the motor car. The foundry continued to function as a major business for the next fifty years but, following the end of the Second World War (during which it made munitions), it found that demand for the manufacture of power drive machinery for the mills, which had represented its main business prior to the war, had been subsumed by new plant manufactured abroad and powered by the diesel electric motor. Harpers had failed to develop other product lines and this, coupled with a general decline in engineering manufacture that affected many Aberdeen enterprises, including the textile, paper, granite and shipbuilding sectors, caused the foundry to finally close its doors around 1960. In the late 1890s, however, all of John Jnr's innovative energies were directed towards motor manufacture, as a result of which he produced the first vehicle in the area to be powered by an internal combustion engine, a two-wheeled tractor that sat between the sheaves of a cart, as well as chassis for Cadillac, Benz and later Ford cars.[47] The bodies were often fitted by another Aberdeen firm, R. & J. Shinnie, Coachbuilders. In the 1890s, Louis too had developed a passion for the motor car and had formed a partnership with John Jnr to build cars at the Craiginches ironworks. Following the 1914–18 Great War, John Jnr's second son Charles (1887–1973) took over the reins of the Aberdeen enterprise and, although the foundry languished, the motor car manufactory prospered. Charlie Harper recalls some of the early years:

My recollections of the motor car go back to the early and middle 'nineties when the 'horseless carriage' was beginning to become the topic of conversation. My father was a firm believer in the future of motoring and I well remember his first attempt at mechanical propulsion when he produced at Craiginches Iron Works what was even then designated a tractor. This was formed of an engine and gear built into the form of a swan-like bird running on rather large wheels with an attachment to which a usual horse-drawn vehicle could be fixed. It really did pull, experimentally, a landau loaned for the occasions by the old firm of R. & J. Shinnie, Coachbuilders, then in Union

120. A 1904 Cadillac at Seafield with Louis at the wheel, his father John in the passenger seat and Louis' family behind: Margaret, Louis (father of the author) and Edward, with family friend George Cruikshank sporting a splendid beard. In front of the bay window are, from left to right, three daughters of Mr Cruickshank and Mrs Alice Harper with new arrival Jessie.

Row. This tractor was the first mechanically propelled vehicle in this district and was an endless source of wonder to me and indeed to all who saw it.

In 1899 the Harper Motor Co. came into being with premises in Bridge Street. (It became a limited company much later.) The following year, the Harper Motor Co. was designated the Benz agent for Scotland. A decade later, in 1911, the company became the 'Ford Main Agent' for the north-east of Scotland, a status it enjoyed until it was taken over by Arnold Clark in 1995. However, the tale of the Harper Motor Co. is another story.

Thus, during the 1890s and the first decade of the twentieth century, the foundry continued to supply power drive machinery to textile and paper mills and to build suspension bridges under Louis' authority. Between the two World Wars its output gradually declined, in common with that of heavy engineering throughout the UK. This decline was felt to be particularly harsh in Aberdeen, which lay some distance from both sources of raw materials and also markets for its products. Charles' main focus, like that of his father, was concentrated on the successful car, tractor and commercial vehicle business, and the manager appointed to run the foundry was allowed to soldier on. It is little wonder that Tony Weller saw scant change in the works by the 1950s (Chapter 6). No doubt Harpers Ltd would have been adversely affected by the depression of the 1930s as the foundry was itself dependent on local industry which suffered decline. However, those who were in work continued to spend money, particularly on new houses, domestic appliances and motor cars. Thus the Harpers group of businesses adapted to the times, but its centre of gravity had moved from one based on manufacturing to that of a service industry.

What of Louis and the bridge business? As a professional engineer in sole practice, Louis was without a partner who could develop and continue the business once he retired. He was obviously very busy in the 1890s and was still advertising bridges in 1916 but there is little evidence that he was active after 1918, when he would have reached the age of 50. The last bridge for which we found definite information was that at Narva, Estonia, built in 1908, although it is possible Louis sent later bridges to Nepal. It may be that Louis' general civil engineering and arhcitectural practice was sufficient to keep him going and, with no prospect of a successor, his focus on the bridge construction arm of the Harpers portfolio waned.

Louis' eldest son Edward joined the Shanghai Police, Louis R., his second son, became a BBC engineer after a spell with Marconi, and his youngest, Douglas, became a commodity trader in Kuala Lumpur with Harrisons, Barker & Co. Ltd. His elder daughter, Margaret, married a doctor and settled in Birmingham, while his younger married daughter died of appendicitis at the age of 27. Did the Harper engineering gene survive? My brother John (b. 1936), son of Louis R., became a mechanical engineer with Babcock & Wilcox, in Renfrew, and his son Neil (b. 1962) joined the same firm. However, my sister Elspeth married a local businessman and I became a surgeon. Nothing lasts for ever.

John Harper of Seafield and his younger son Louis made for an interesting contrast. John, the 'lad o'pairts' from humble origins, epitomised the successful self-made man of the late Victorian era. Born into a large family, John Snr had left the certainty of the farm at an early age and made his own way in life far from home. His was a remarkable career. He came from farm-labouring stock, was self-educated after the age of 9, worked as a gardener, fencer and ironfounder, and subsequently as a bridge builder for royalty and throughout the Empire, became a prosperous businessman, and served as a Justice of the Peace, Burgess of Guild and local politician. John was described as having 'a bright and breezy disposition',[4] retained the common touch and enjoyed a reputation for helping those less fortunate than himself. Neither was he above rolling up his sleeves himself in his later years to do some of the more menial tasks associated with bridge building.

In his autobiography, written in his 80s, Alexander Falconer Murison recalls his schooldays at Aberdeen Grammar School, and particularly a highly successful prize-giving ceremony, which resulted in his receipt of a succession of book prizes:

> The 'Visitation' Exercise was specially connected with the annual visit of the patrons (the Lord Provost, Magistrates, and Councillors of the City) on Prize Giving Day. As the magnates were filing down from the platform, Councillor Harper genially bent down to me and said, 'Have you ordered a Pickford [a wagon of the Pickford company of public carriers]?'

Louis, by contrast with his father, despite his much older stepsister and brother, was brought up virtually as an only child by parents comfortably

121. Louis Harper with his son Douglas, around 1922.

and entered the second year of his secondary schooling at Aberdeen Grammar School. He was a keen gymnast in his youth and remained a fit, good-looking man, with a distinguished air – it was said he even moved a gear lever with a certain panache. A tale of Louis climbing a rope to the ceiling of the Aberdeen Music Hall in a competition inspires an image that revisits me regularly when I should be concentrating on the *andante*.

In 1906 Louis moved his office from 115 Union Street (the previous home of John Harper, where Louis had been born in 1868) to Seafield. Not for him his father's life of involvement in the city's civic and business life. Around the age of 50, Louis retired and Harpers ceased to make his suspension bridges.

In his long semi-retirement, Louis journeyed far and wide, at a time when a good journey from Aberdeen to London might take three days. In thirty-five years he covered well over half a million miles and he kept a complete record of all his travels. Yet he remained essentially a private person with a small circle of close friends. His plans, handwriting, artwork and diary all attest to a meticulous nature. He died in 1940, shortly after hearing of the tragic death of his son, Douglas, in an aircraft crash at Bali in the Philippines. His wife and his daughter Jessie had predeceased him.

Louis had taken up the mantle of his father's bridge-building enterprise at a young age and undoubtedly made a success of it. He brought it up to date and developed the double opposed curve system of suspension. The bridges continued to be exported to all five continents, as they had in his father's time, and several survive today, still serving the communities in which they were erected. In their time, the Harpers, father and son, were among the leading exponents of the light steel rope suspension bridge worldwide.

off in a country house in which he was to spend his entire life, apart from a few years. Whereas John Snr had made his own way from a young age, emerging as a natural leader with an outgoing personality, Louis was sent to a prep school in Kent for a year in 1880–81. Judging from the letters Louis wrote home from school, he was a rather lonely and insecure teenager, whose one redeeming feature in the eyes of his fellow pupils was an aptitude for cricket. Louis returned to Aberdeen in 1881

APPENDIX 1

HARPER SUSPENSION FOOTBRIDGES

Bridges in use in 2014 in **bold**

Bridge	River	Country	Year Erected	Year Down	Span ft (m)	Width ft (m)	Evidence	Page
BRITISH ISLES								
Abercynon	Taff	Wales	c. 1900	1942			definite	91
Aberlour	**Spey**	**Scotland**	**1900**		**287 (87.48)**		**partial**	**96**
Aboyne	Dee	Scotland	1871	?1913	300 (91.44)		definite	53
Ardnacarrig	Bandon	Eire	1890	1927	120 (36.58)	4 (1.22)	definite	71
Birkhall	**Muick**	**Scotland**	**1880**		**60 (18.29)**	**3 (0.91)**	**definite**	**49**
Burnhervie	Don	Scotland	c. 1880	1979	100 (30.05)		definite	59
Cambus o' May	**Dee**	**Scotland**	**1905**		**164 (49.98)**	**4 (1.22)**	**partial**	**95**
Craighall	Ericht	Scotland	1886	c. 1955	90 (27.43)		definite	62
Crathorne	Leven	England	1888	1930	55 (16.76)	4 (1.22)	definite	67
Cromdale	Spey (i)	Scotland	1881	1894	195 (59.44)		definite	60
Cromdale	Spey (ii)	Scotland	1894	1927			probable	84
Dee near Chester	Dee	England	1887–93				possible	154
Doveridge	Dove	England	1898	1945			definite	90
Dundee	Caledonian Rlwy	Scotland	1872		55 (16.76)		definite	46
Falkirk	Carron	Scotland	1893	2014	90 (27.43)	4(1.22)	definite	80
Feugh Lodge	**Feugh**	**Scotland**	**1893**		**100 (30.05)**	**4(1.22)**	**definite**	**72**
Glentanar (March Burn)	Tanar	Scotland	1871	after 1927	100 (30.05)		definite	53
Glen Tanar (Tanarmouth)	Tanar	Scotland	1871	1939	100 (30.05)		definite	51
Glentanar (6 Others)	Tanar	Scotland	c. 1870				probable	53
Grimsby 1	Freshney	England	1894	1972?	50 (15.24)	4 (1.22)	definite	82
Grimsby 2	Freshney	England	1894	1970	50 (15.24)	4 (1.22)	definite	82
Grimsby 3	Freshney	England	1894	1970	35 (10.67)	4 (1.22)	definite	82
Holme	GNR	England	<1887		80 (24.38)	6 (1.83)	definite	56
Jubilee	Nairn	Scotland	1887	1915	100 (30.05)		definite	64

Bridge	River	Country	Year Erected	Year Down	Span ft (m)	Width ft (m)	Evidence	Page
Keswick	Greta	England	1898	1979	90 (27.43)	4 (1.22)	definite	89
Lincoln	GNR	England	1893		70 (21.34)		definite	70
Monymusk	Don	Scotland	1879	2005	107 (32.61)	4 (1.22)	definite	57
Nairn	Nairn	Scotland	1887	1915	100 (30.05)		definite	64
Newquay	**Island**	**England**	*c.* **1900**		**100 (30.48)**	**4 (1.22)**	**definite**	**92**
Offord	GNR	England	1887				definite	64
Sellack	**Wye**	**England**	**1895**		**190 (57.91)**	**6 (1.83)**	**definite**	**87**
Shocklach	Dee	England	1871	1935	160 (48.77)		definite	54
Tentham	Trent	England	1893	*c.* 1935	70 (21.34)		definite	82
INDIA								
Baroda		India	1898	*c.* 1980	300 (91.44) (91)	8 (2.44)	definite	103
Bombay		India	1895		210 (64.01)	6 (1.83)	definite	102
Jumna	Jumna Canal	India	1898	1942	200 (60.96)	8 (2.44)	definite	103
Unknown		India	*c.* 1898		300 (91.44)	8 (2.44)	definite	
Unknown		India					definite	
NEPAL								
Chobar	Bagmati	Nepal	1903		130 (39.62)	4 (1.22)	definite	121
Kohkani	Bagmati	Nepal	1903	1965	400 (121.92)		probable	119
Kulekhani		Nepal	*c.* 1900				possible	119
Mangaltar	Rosi	Nepal	1907		130 (39.62)		definite	133
Sangutar	Likhu	Nepal	1907		130 (39.62)		definite	136
Trisuli Bazar		Nepal	1900	1972	120 (36.58)	4 (1.22)	definite	125
Sundari		Nepal	1901–03		280 (85.34)	4 (1.22)	definite	123
Unknown		Nepal	1901–03		110 (33.53)	4 (1.22)	definite	114
Unknown		Nepal	1901–03		150 (45.72)	4 (1.22)	definite	114
Unknown		Nepal	1901–03		90 (27.43)	4 (1.22)	definite	114
Unknown		Nepal	1901–03		180 (54.86)	4 (1.22)	definite	114
ESTONIA, FALKLAND ISLANDS, SOUTH AFRICA								
Tsomo	Tsomo	RSA	1898	*c.* 1970	120 (36.58)	6 (1.8)	definite	106
Krenholm	Narva	Estonia	1908	1944	260 (79.25)	6 (1.83)	definite	108
Darwin Harbour		FID	1887–93	1913			probable	110
West Indies			1898		110 (33.53)		definite	110

APPENDIX 2

THE

HARPER SUSPENSION BRIDGE

FOR LIGHT TRAFFIC ONLY.

A Unique Specialty, combining Moderate Cost, Easy Transit, Simplicity of Erection, Elegance and Strength.

PRICE

for the Complete Bridge, similar to this Photograph, fitted and marked ready for Erection, and packed for Export, everything being included except timber and cement.

Span in feet.	Four feet wide. £	Five feet wide. £	Six feet wide. £
50	130	145	175
60	145	160	190
70	160	175	205
80	175	190	220
90	190	205	235
100	205	220	250
110	220	235	265
120	235	250	280
130	250	265	295
140	265	280	310
150	280	295	325
160	295	310	340
170	310	325	355
180	325	340	371
190	340	355	388
200	355	370	406
210	370	386	425
220	385	403	445
230	400	421	466
240	415	440	488
250	430	460	511
260	445	481	534
270	460	503	558
280	475	525	583
290	490	548	609
300	505	572	636

When remittance is sent with order a discount of 7½ per cent. may be deducted; otherwise the price is nett cash in London against B/L.

ILLUSTRATION OF A HARPER BRIDGE ERECTED IN INDIA, 210 FEET SPAN × 5 FEET WIDE.

DELIVERY

F. O. B. any important seaport in the Kingdom, the following being an approximate guide to further freight and transit for a bridge with platform four feet wide.

Span in feet.	Total dead-weight cwts.	Heaviest piece being lbs.	Except 4 ropes each cwts.
50	45	88	2¾
60	48	88	3
70	52	91	3¼
80	57	94	3½
90	63	98	3¾
100	70	103	4
110	77	109	4½
120	84	116	5
130	91	124	5½
140	98	133	6
150	106	143	6½
160	114	154	7
170	122	166	7¾
180	130	179	8½
190	138	193	9¼
200	146	208	10
210	154	225	10¾
220	162	244	11½
230	171	265	12¼
240	180	288	13
250	189	314	14
260	199	343	15
270	210	375	16½
280	222	411	18
290	236	453	20
300	253	503	23

If the platform is required five feet wide add 10 per cent. to above weights, and if six feet wide add 20 per cent. to above weights.

ERECTION ON THE SITE IS A MOST SIMPLE MATTER,

because the parts are accurately made and fitted ready for erection, and can be put together expeditiously, under the superintendence of an intelligent workman, without the slightest difficulty, he being guided by the specially prepared detailed drawings and instructions which accompany the materials, including a list of the necessary timber for flooring. Special tools are also sent for the erection.

HOW TO DETERMINE THE SPAN

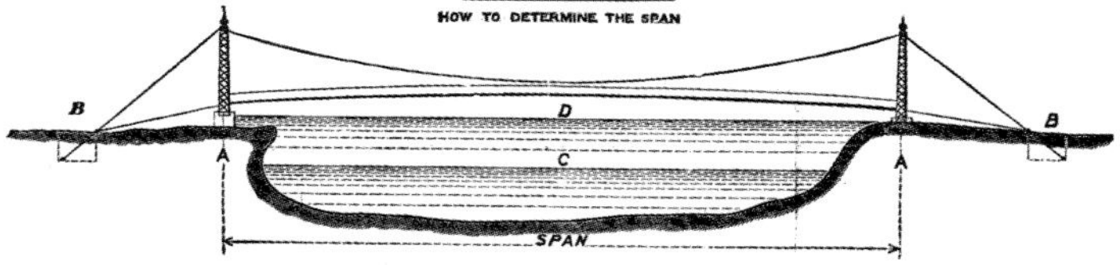

THE ORDER must be accompanied by a cross section of the site according to above sample sketch, together with the following information :—

1.—The required span in feet between the pillars, which should be kept well back on the banks, as shown by A A, with sufficient distance behind for the anchorage B B.
2.—Level of ground surface A A and B B as well as the ordinary level (C) and highest flood level (D), by which the elevation of the bridge is determined.
3.—The nature of the banks A A and B B, whether earth or rock, so that suitable fixings may be sent.
4.—If these particulars are explicit, the bridge will be despatched in six weeks or thereby.

GENERAL DESCRIPTION OF BRIDGE.

FOUNDATIONS.—The foundation anchor blocks are formed of cement concrete, in which are embedded the rails and eye-rods for attachment of main ropes.

STEEL LATTICE PILLARS.—The four pillars of the bridge are formed of open steel lattice-work, and are set on stone or concrete blocks prepared for them. Each pair of pillars is connected near the top by lattice-work, and each pillar is surmounted with cast-iron saddle and neat finial. These pillars are sent complete if specially ordered, but otherwise in pieces for easy transit, with the necessary rivets and service bolts.

ROPES.—The ropes are made from the best patent galvanised steel wire; the core of the rope also being of wire to prevent elongation after erection. At the ends of each rope are secured special castings, through which staple screws are inserted, and the whole is attached to the eye-rod in concrete anchor block already referred to.

VERTICAL RODS.—The vertical rods are made of solid steel galvanised, spaced two feet apart, and are secured to the suspending and platform ropes by means of a special clip. Each rod is calculated to a sixteenth of an inch in length, so that each may bear its own load, and preserve the true dip and camber.

FLOORING.—The flooring of timber consists of crossbearers, which vary in thickness according to the width of footway, and these rest on, and are secured to, the platform ropes by means of hook bolts. The flooring, preferably tongued and grooved, is laid down longitudinally and nailed to the crossbearers. Skirting on edge is then run along either side of the platform, and is securely bolted down to the flooring and crossbearers.

LATTICE PANELLING.—The sides of the bridge are guarded with strong corrugated diamond wire panelling, which is secured to the vertical rods, skirting and pillars.

TIGHTENING.—The tightening of the bridge is done by means of the staple screws, at eight different points, so that the bridge is rendered virtually rigid at the finish. The platform has a camber or arch, varying from one to five feet high, according to the span.

STRENGTH.—The strength of the bridge is undoubted, as it will bear a load on the platform of 160 lb. to the square foot distributed, or equal to about twice the weight of all the people who could stand on it at one time. When circumstances demand a greater margin of safety, the strength can be increased to any desired extent at a *pro rata* increase of price.

LOUIS HARPER, A.M.I.C.E., ABERDEEN, SCOTLAND.

Contractor to the India Office, Colonial and other Foreign Governments.

APPENDIX 3

SUSPENSION BRIDGES IN INDIA

All text from *Suspension Bridges in India*, Hoare, A. (Bombay: Turner, Hoare & Co., 1900):

Having now given a brief specification of the suspension bridges made by Louis Harper, we will proceed to the simplicity of erection of such a bridge; and the photos here reproduced, taken by Mr Arthur Hoare during the construction of a bridge, will greatly facilitate this explanation.

Our illustration on page 2 shows the abutments of the bridge being made and the foundations put in. The scaffolding, which the natives are seen erecting, is to assist them in hoisting the lattice pillars in position and keeping them there while the strain is being placed on the ropes.

It may be mentioned, incidentally, that the complete drawings, furnished at the time the bridge is ordered, enable the work on foundations and abutments to be carried out by an intelligent 'mistri' or native foreman.

The illustrations on pages 4 & 5 clearly represent the erection of the lattice columns. That on page 6 also gives a view of the 300ft nullah which the bridge is designed to span.

After the pillars are placed in position and strongly guyed, the platform or lower ropes are uncoiled and stretched across the water and threaded through the eye of the anchor rods, and the ends are then attached to the steel casting supplied for this purpose. These ropes can then be drawn taut by screwing up at each end.

The next operation consists of placing the cross-bearers on the ropes and utilising the hooks, provided for this purpose, to keep them in position. The illustration on page 8 shows coolies underneath the bridge, hauling up the cross-bearers which have been floated down the stream. At the time this particular bridge was erected, the river was low enough to allow the men to work in the bed, but even when rivers are in flood, or non-fordable, the hauling up of the cross-bearers presents no difficulties, as it can either be done from boats or the cross-bearers can be brought on the bridge from one end.

The suspending ropes can now be fixed. Each rope is marked in red with the precise position that each vertical rod should occupy. It is, of course, a matter for the erector to decide which is the best way of getting these ropes to the top of the pillars and laid on the saddle. In order to ensure getting these ropes in their proper places, the most satisfactory is to pass one end of the rope at a time, run it over the saddle and down to anchor iron rods. When this has been done at both ends, the screws can then be tightened up until the large red mark on the suspending rope is drawn on to its correct position on the saddle.

Our illustration on page 10 shows the next operation of fixing the vertical rod between the two ropes. These vertical rods should be carefully unpacked and placed along the bank according to their different lengths, and a man should be told off to hand them up to the fixers and be responsible for giving out the right lengths. In attaching the verticals, a start should be made from the lattice pillars at one end, the men working towards the centre, hooking the verticals on to the red marks on the suspension ropes and leaving the lower end free.

Having arrived at the centre, they again commence at the other end and work towards the middle.

Commencing now from the centre, the verticals can be hooked on to the lower or platform ropes, and to do this a block and tackle will be required to draw the two ropes together.

The vertical rods having all been fixed in position, the bridge may now be tightened. This should be done slowly and with care, so that equal strains are placed on all the ropes.

The flooring on the bridge will now be laid down and securely nailed or screwed to the cross-bearers, the skirting being neatly done to give the platform a finished appearance. This is shown in the illustration on page 12.

The last operation to be performed is that of fixing the lattice wire-work, which forms the necessary protection at the sides of the bridge. The approaches to the bridge may, of course, be prepared in any way desired, either in wood, masonry or earth banking, as in the illustration on page 14.

The bridge is now complete; and a glance at our illustration will show that, though simple in design and easily constructed, its symmetrical lines are perfect to a degree and the bridge appears neat, rigid and elegant.

An improvement has been recently introduced by Mr Harper for tightening up the vertical rods, should they become slightly elongated either in transit or owing to uneven expansion. This is Mr H.C. Matheson's eccentric ring, shown in the illustrations herewith. This ring or washer is threaded on to the lower or platform ropes before the verticals are hooked on to it, and each vertical rod clamps the washer instead of the rope. The bridge is erected with the washer having its smaller thickness at the bottom as in Figure a. Should any vertical rods become slightly elongated, by means of a special key, the eccentric ring can be turned round so as to slightly lengthen the distance between the ropes as in Figure b. This washer has been found to admirably answer its purpose.

Turner, Hoare & Co.
Engineers and Contractors
Bombay

Sole Agents for
Mr Louis Harper, Assoc., MICE
Bridge Contractor,
Aberdeen

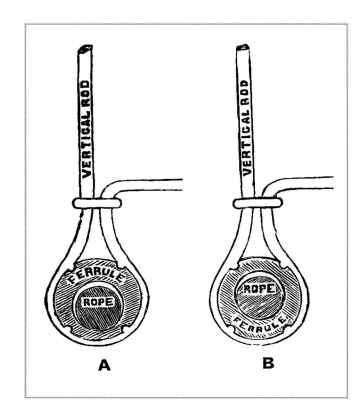

APPENDIX 4

HARPER BRIDGES IN THE BRITISH ISLES

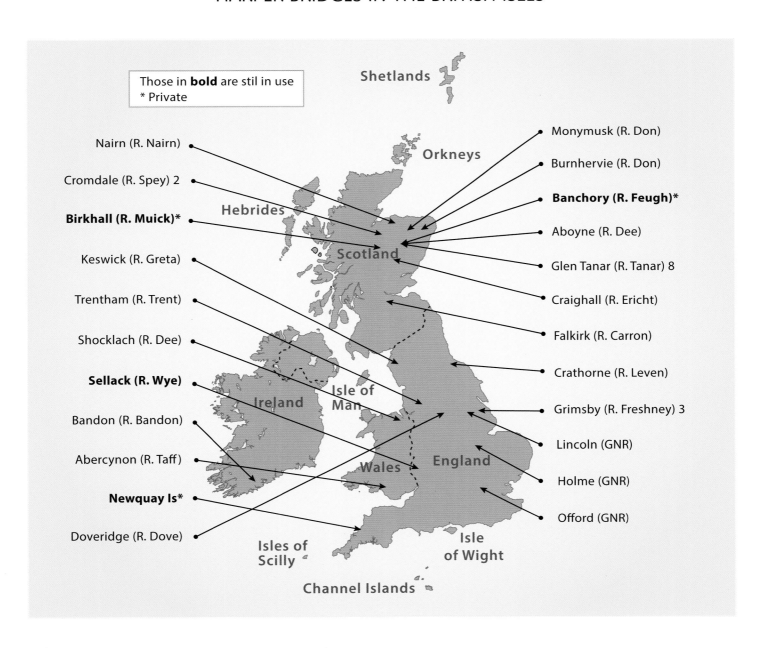

Those in **bold** are stil in use
* Private

Shetlands

Orkneys

Hebrides

Scotland

Ireland

Isle of Man

Wales

England

Isles of Scilly

Isle of Wight

Channel Islands

Nairn (R. Nairn)

Cromdale (R. Spey) 2

Birkhall (R. Muick)*

Keswick (R. Greta)

Trentham (R. Trent)

Shocklach (R. Dee)

Sellack (R. Wye)

Bandon (R. Bandon)

Abercynon (R. Taff)

Newquay Is*

Doveridge (R. Dove)

Monymusk (R. Don)

Burnhervie (R. Don)

Banchory (R. Feugh)*

Aboyne (R. Dee)

Glen Tanar (R. Tanar) 8

Craighall (R. Ericht)

Falkirk (R. Carron)

Crathorne (R. Leven)

Grimsby (R. Freshney) 3

Lincoln (GNR)

Holme (GNR)

Offord (GNR)

NOTES

1. Wyness F., Personal Communication (1960).
2. *Census, 1851* (Register House, Edinburgh).
3. *Census, 1841* (Register House, Edinburgh).
4. *Our Portrait* (The Northern Figaro, 1886).
5. W. Hamish Fraser, Clive H. Lee, *Aberdeeon, 1800–2000: A New History* (Tuckwell Press Ltd, 2000).
6. Alexander Keith, *A Thousand Years of Aberdeen* (Aberdeen University Press,1972).
7. Carter I., *Farm Life in Northeast Scotland 1840–1914*. 2003 ed. (Edinburgh: John Donald, 2003).
8. Murray C., *Hamewith* (London: Constable, 1909).
9. In Memorium. p.67 (Aberdeen: Campbell, 1906).
10. Harper J., inventors, *Improvements in Pillars and Apparatus for Straining Wire*, UK patent 3031 (1863).
11. Rowell J., inventors, *Pillars and Apparatus for Straining Wire*, UK patent 2516 (1862).
12. Rowell J., inventors, *Improvements in the Manufacture and Con-struction of Fences, Part of which are also applicable to the Manufacture and Construction of Gate Posts, and to Poles and Posts used for Telegraph and Signal Purposes, and for Stretching Telegraph Wires*, UK patent 2192 (1863).
13. Harper D.R., Day T.M., *The Nineteenth Century Suspension Footbridges of Harpers of Aberdeen,* 32:21-33 (Industrial Archaeological Review, 2010).
14. Hunter S.W.W., *Notes from the Indian Empire; its Peoples, History and Products.* 3rd ed. p.482 (London: W.H. Allen, 1893).
15. Stevenson R., *Description of Bridges of Suspension,* 237–256 (The Edinburgh Philosophical Journal 1821; 10 October).
16. Peters T.F., *Transitions in Engineering: Guillaume Henri Dufour and the Early Nineteenth Century Cable Suspension Bridges* p.14 (Basel, Boston: Birkhauser Verlag, 1987).
17. Kawada K., *History of the Modern Suspension Bridge* pp.1 (American Society of Civil Engineers, 2010).
18. Sayenga, D., *A History of Wrought-Iron Wire Suspension Bridge Cables: Proceedings of an International Conference to Celebrate the 150th Anniversary of the Wheeling Suspension Bridge* (West Virginia University Press, 1999).
19. Ruddock, T., *Blacksmith Bridges in Scotland and Ireland 1816–1834: Proceedings of an International Conference to Celebrate the 150th Anniversary of the Wheeling Suspension Bridge* (West Virginia University Press, 1999).

20. Peters T.F., *Transitions in Engineering: Guillaume Henri Dufour and the Early Nineteenth Century Cable Suspension Bridges* pp.36 (Basel, Boston: Birkhauser Verlag, 1987).

21. Robert Hall, *History of Galashiels* pp.92–3. (Galashiels: The Galashiels Manufacturers' Corporation. Alexander Walker & Sons, 1898).

22. Robert Hall, *History of Galashiels* pp.93–4. (The Galashiels Manufacturers' Corporation. Alexander Walker & Sons, 1898).

23. Drewry C.S., *A Memoir of Suspension Bridges Comprising the History of their Origin and Progress* p.27 (London: Longman, Rees, Orme, Brown, Green & Longman, 1832).

24. Pendet S., *The Solution of Tension* in *A Span of Bridges* p.206 (Hopkins H.J., editor. 1st ed. New York: Praeger, 1970).

25. Dupit MdCHR., *Rapport de la commission d'enquete nommee par arrete de M. le prefet de Maine-et-Loire, en date du 20 avril 1850, pour rechercher les causes et les circonstances qui ont amene la chute de pont suspendu de Basse-Chaine. Annales des Ponts et Chausee* (1850; III).

26. Serrel E.W., *The Applicability of Suspension Bridges to railways* (Amer Railway J 1853; 2626 March).

27. Drewry C.S., *A Memoir of Suspension Bridges: Comprising the History of their Origin and Progress* (London: Longman, Rees, Orme, Brown, Green & Longman, 1832).

28. Hume J.R., *Scottish Suspension Bridges,* 8:91–104 (Scottish Archaeological Forum, 1977).

29. O'Connor C., Personal Communication (2007).

30. McCullough D., *The Great Bridge* p.162 (New York: Simon & Schuster, 2012).

31. Fouin F.L.P., *The Brooks Era. Glen Tanar: Valley of Echoes and Hidden Treasurers* pp.141–50 (2009).

32. W. Hamish Fraser, Clive H. Lee, *Aberdeen, 1800–2000: A New History* pp.33–4(Tuckwell Press Ltd., 2000).

33. McConnochie AI. Bennachie, *Aberdeen* p.30 (James G. Bisset Ltd, 1890).

34. William Watson, *Glimpses of Auld Lang Syne* p.282 (Aberdeen: Aberdeen University Press, 1905).

35. *Strathspey Estate Papers* (National Archives of Scotland. GD226. 1892).

36. *Strathspey Estate Papers* (National Archives of Scotland GD227. 1892).

37. Crawley, J., *The Great North Railway in Focus* p.18 (Wellingsborough: Wharton W.D., 2001).

38. *Aberdeen Street Directory* (Aberdeen: The Post Office, 1887).

39. Harper L. *The Harper Suspension Bridge* (Aberdeen: L. Harper, 1900).

40. *Visit of the Institution of Civil Engineers to Aberdeen pp.*108–9 (The Engineer, 1907).

41. Devine T.M., *To the Ends of the Earth: Scotland's Global Diaspora* pp.56–84 (London: Allen Lane, 2011).

42. Hunter S.W.W., *Notes from the Indian Empire; its Peoples, History and Products*, 3rd ed. p.456 (London: W.H. Allen, 1893).

43. Hunter S.W.W., *Notes from the Indian Empire; its Peoples, History and Products*, 3rd ed. p.456 (London: W.H. Allen, 1893).

44. Livingstone W.P., *Christina Forsyth of Fingoland: The Story of the Loneliest Woman in Africa* (Nabu Press, 2009).

45. Herman A., *How the Scots Invented the Modern World* p.374 (New York: Three Rivers Press, 2001).

46. Landon P., *Nepal* p.36 (London: Constable, 1928).

47. Northey W.B., *Land of the Gurkhas* (Cambridge: W. Heffer & Sons, 1925).

48. Landon P., *Nepal* pp.199–200 (London: Constable, 1928).

49. Landon P., *Nepal* pp.179–80 (London: Constable, 1928).

50. Landon P., *Nepal* p.13 (London: Constable, 1928).

51. Ward M., *The First Cars: The Dawn of the Motoring Era in Aberdeenshire 1895–1905* (Alford, Aberdeenshire: Grampian Transport Museum, 2000).

INDEX

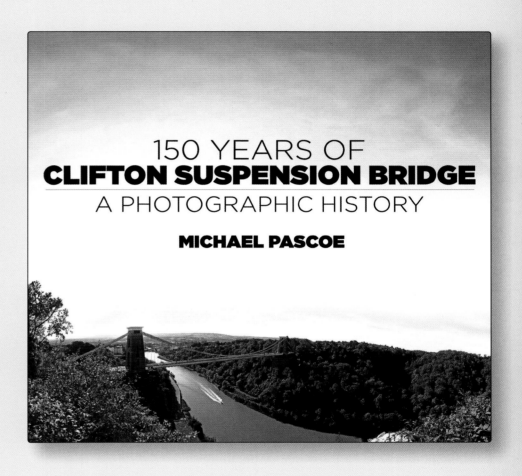

Brunel's Kingdom: In the Footsteps of Britain's Greatest Engineer

JOHN CHRISTOPHER

Brunel's Kingdom is the story of of the great engineer told through the works he left behind. More than just a biography, the book is designed to be used as a guide so that the reader can, if they wish, visit any of the relics, sites and structures featured within the book. This is an entertaining, readable and informative look at Brunel's life and career.

978 0 7509 6306 0

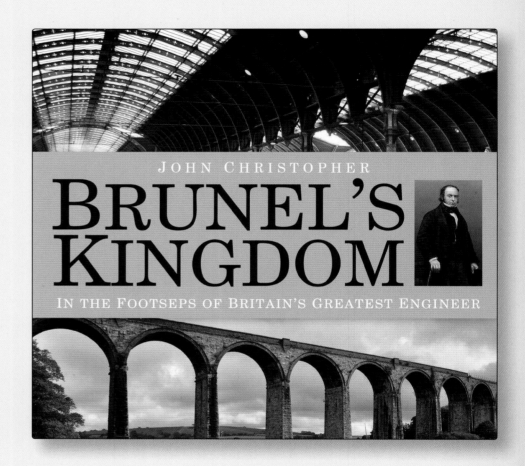

The Beautiful Railway Bridge of the Silvery Tay: Reinvestigating the Tay Bridge Disaster of 1879

PETER LEWIS

The Tay Bridge disaster of 28 December 1879 shocked and horrified Victorian society – a whole train and at least seventy-five passengers and crew were lost. This book describes the reinvestigation of the disaster and its shocking conclusions. In the aftermath, engineers had to convince the travelling public that they could build safely, and the new bridge was the first result of their efforts.

978 0 7524 3160 4

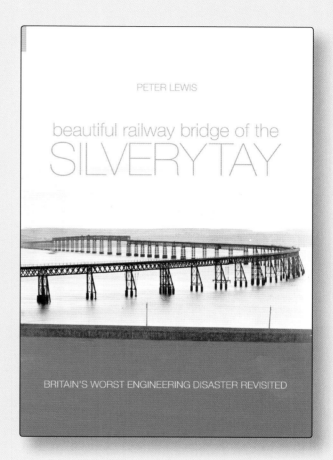

Visit our website and discover thousands of other History Press books.
www.thehistorypress.co.uk

The History Press

Guide to Urban Engineering: Infrastructure and Technology in the Modern Landscape

CLAIRE BARRATT AND IAN WHITELAW

Spotter's guides traditionally focus on the natural world but if we are to understand the modern landscape it is vital to recognise its manmade features. *Guide to Urban Engineering* provides non-specialist readers with an introduction to the technology that underpins modern life. Each chapter explores various engineering features and structures, detailing what they are, what they do, how they do it, and, most importantly, how to identify them.

978 0 7524 6997 3

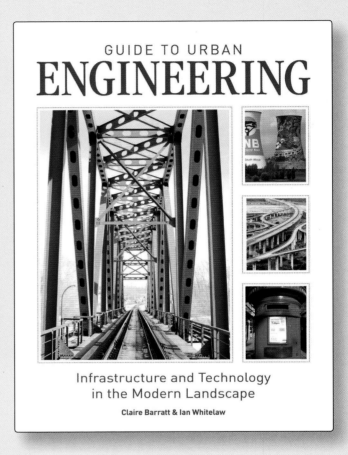

GUIDE TO URBAN
ENGINEERING

Infrastructure and Technology
in the Modern Landscape

Claire Barratt & Ian Whitelaw